For Such a Time as This?

Dawn Densmore-Parent

Cover Design by: Tamara Smith, UVM Print and Mail, VT

Scriptures are from the Holy Bible, King James Version

©Copyright 2020

ISBN: 978-1-7342353-1-9

INTRODUCTION

When we walk in love towards God and one another we create a foundation for the Lord to reveal Himself to us in extraordinary ways. Serving God has blessings for believers right now, as well as eternal rewards. *For I know the thoughts that I think toward you, saith the Lord, thoughts of peace, and not of evil, to give you an expected end* (Jeremiah 29:11). *And ye shall seek me, and find me, when ye shall search for me with all your heart* (Jeremiah 29:13).

2022 FORWARD: This book **"For Such A Time as This?"** was written in 2020 during the COVID pandemic. The cover features the Moon with its reflection in the water from June 5, 2020 which was a Strawberry Full Moon. My first book, **"DIVINE ENCOUNTERS: The Reality of God, Angels and Demons"** also contains the image of a full moon on the cover. The reason for featuring a full moon on both covers, is because on the night of June 28, 1980, an event occurred with the Moon which reflects the times in which we live. Now that event of 1980 is remarkably similar to another event that occurred the night of June 27, 2022.

On June 27, 2022, while I was re-reading "For Such a Time as This?" my husband Fabien came to our back French door and said, "You need to come out and see something!" I put this book down to see what he wanted to show me. As I joined him outside on our deck, he said, "There is a **Super Strawberry Full Moon** tonight! It is the largest moon because it is closest to the earth and that will not happen again for a long time!" As we gazed at that moon, I said, "Do you know what this is an image of Fabien? This is the cover of my **book "For Such a Time as This?"** He replied, "Oh, yes I see it!" I asked, "Do you know what book I was reading when you came to get me?" He said, "No." I replied, "I was re-reading "For Such a Time as This?" and I was in the chapter about the rapture!" Both of us were amazed. When I got back inside my home, I looked up the verse in my 1980 bible that I had marked to check the date regarding John 14:21 from the night of June 28, 1980.

On June 28, 1980, my first husband Jim Densmore, Jr. had also been extremely excited about a full moon and had come to tell me, "There is a full moon tonight!" He repeated "Yes a full moon". I was not excited at all! But that night, I awoke to see a BIG full moon in the window. That night as I gazed at that moon, as I was thanking Jesus for my salvation, suddenly the real 'face' of Jesus appeared to me in the moon. I lifted my hand and waved' and said 'Hi Jesus!" As I gazed at him, I thought this is crazy! I cannot be seeing Jesus's face in the moon! I closed my eyes and then opened them. There was just the moon. I was relieved! I told the Lord, "Wow, I thought I saw your face in the moon, but I was mistaken! But just as suddenly as before Jesus's face appeared AGAIN.! The second time he smiled a half-smile at me and then, as I watched, his face just disappeared. When I had prayed for confirmation, I had opened to John 14:21 and wrote the date 6/28/80 in the margin. The next morning, I shared what happened with my husband Jim. He said, "We'll talk about this later!" But we never did talk about it ever again. I kept the reality of this occurrence to myself for 32 years. My life moved on, we parted and then divorced. Jim went to help his parents and I worked to help my parents. I purchased my home in 2004 and my Dad came to live with me in 2008 (he went to be with the Lord December 1, 2015). Each night I would talk with my Dad and share my faith with him. One night he told me, 'You ought to write a book!?" I had never considered writing before but decided to just write down my experiences which became my first book entitled, **"DIVINE ENCOUNTERS: The Reality of God, Angels, and Demons"** in which I included this occurrence.

After the experience of June 27, 2022, I decided to just check to see if the full moon in 1980 was a Strawberry Full Moon. I learned both moons on June 28, 1980 and June 27, 2022 were Full Strawberry Moons; however, the **June 27, 2022 moon was a SUPER FULL Strawberry Moon**, which made me remember these verses:

"And there shall be signs in the sun, and in the moon, and in the stars; and upon the earth distress of nations, with perplexity; the sea and the waves roaring; Men's hearts failing them for fear, and for looking after those things which are coming on the earth: for the powers of heaven shall be shaken. And then shall they see the Son of man coming in a cloud with power and great glory" (Luke 21:25-27).

Jesus came, died, and rose again that we might have eternal life which is forever. I believe we are the generation that is living in what is known as the 'last days' before the return of the Lord in the air to gather his Bride in the clouds. I encourage you to make sure you have accepted the Lord Jesus Christ and asked for His forgiveness and to come into your life. Each of us will stand before The Lord Jesus Christ to give an account of our lives. On that day we will be glad that His Blood has cleansed us and redeemed us and that we said, "Lord, forgive me and save my soul." On that day, 'born again' will be a very GOOD thing! Between now and then, we each have an opportunity, **'For Such a Time as This!"**. Let us choose to live in obedience to the Lord's commands, to love God and to love one another more than we love this current world. *Lord, may we willing pick up our 'cross' and follow You, because 'soon' and very soon, we are going to see the King! Amen, even so Come Lord Jesus!*

FROM WICKOPEDIA: The supermoon of November 14, 2016, was the closest full occurrence since January 26, 1948, and will not be surpassed until November 25, 2034. The closest full supermoon of the 21st century will occur on December 6, 2052.

Contents

Chapter	Title	Page
Chapter 1	For such a time as this? Last Days	7
Chapter 2	Intervene, Intervene, Intervene	25
Chapter 3	Deliver, Deliver, Deliver	31
Chapter 4	Recover, Recover, Recover	35
Chapter 5	Redeem, Redeem, Redeem	41
Chapter 6	Restore, Restore, Restore	45
Chapter 7	Spiritual Rest	49
Chapter 8	Pray	53
Chapter 9	Yielded	57
Chapter 10	Singlemindedness	61
Chapter 11	Be Still	65
Chapter 12	White Linen	69
Chapter 13	Walls of Protection	73
Chapter 14	Please God	81

Chapter 15	83
Have Faith	83
Chapter 16	87
Wait	87
Chapter 17	89
Don't Quit	89
Chapter 18	93
Abide	93
Chapter 19	97
Look Ahead	97
Chapter 20	103
Remembrance	103
Chapter 21	109
Silver and Gold	109
Chapter 22	113
The Overcomer	113
Chapter 23	127
Vessels Only	127
Chapter 24	133
The Key	133

Chapter 1

For such a time as this? Last Days

"Ye have heaped together treasures for the last days. "

James 5:3

What was true in the past, is true for believers today. We were made by God from the dust of the earth, and to 'dust' we shall return. The key question is what should be our ultimate purpose while we are alive on earth? The Bible answers that question. We are created beings with free will choice. The purpose for those who choose to believe in a God who created all things, while they are on earth, is to become 'vessels of honor' for His use. Every lifetime contains the opportunity to look forward to 'eternal life' as well as begin to experience the presence of God with us, in the midst of us. Those who become yielded, prayerful, and obedient to the leading of God's Holy Spirit, have the opportunity to become one with each other. The Bible's spiritual wisdom provides us with the tools and with guidance to live such a life. When we choose to make God first in our life, God's Holy Spirit assists us in loving others as we love ourselves. It is during the 'trials' of life that we are refined. Trials allow us to grow in our relationship with the Lord, as well as with each other. The entire world is actually God's 'stage' created for us. The 'things' of this world are His 'prop's that are used to enable us to live in harmony with God and each other. The 'true treasure' of life is not 'things' or 'wealth' but in connecting with the very presence of God's Holy Spirit.

God promises to give His Holy Spirit to whosoever calls upon His Holy Name.

It is during 'Life's unexpected events' that the contents of what is in our 'vessel' appear. These squeeze what is 'inside of us' to come out of us. The trials of this life: suffering, pain, and even death itself - for those who choose to believe in God - all have silver linings in eternity. These very 'things' mysteriously produce God's 'sweetness' within our eternal souls: patience, love, joy, peace, longsuffering, gentleness, goodness, faith – these are the 'fruit of God's Holy Spirit (Galatians 5: 22-23). But the trials of this life can also squeeze out 'fear' which then focuses concern on ourselves over others. This can create unbelief in a God who would 'allow' bad things to happen; then any event can cause us to experience feelings of hatred, anger, which in turn, can produce harsh words, slander, etc. These things leave us void of an ability to forgive one another. With this in mind, let us examine events that are worthy of our attention: The HMS Titanic, 9/11, as well as the fallout created by the unexpected COVID19 virus. Can true accounts from the Titanic and from the 9/11 collapse of the New York City Twin Towers provide important information on how to live, 'In Such a Time as This?" These events reflect how very important it is for us to work together, as well as to listen to one anther with respect.

The Book "Futility"

In 1898, the book, "*Futility*" was written by Morgan Robertson. Originally titled, "*The Wreck of the Titan*" it is about a ship called Titan. Fourteen years later, in 1912, the HMS Titanic would mirror Robertson's story.

The HMS Titanic

The owners and builders of the HMS titanic rejected plans that called for as many as 64 lifeboats. The agreed upon number of 20 lifeboats held half of the 2,228 people aboard. An employee of the White Star Line declared at its launch:

"Not even God himself could sink this ship."

Launch of the Titanic, *May 31, 1911*

The HMS Titanic did sink in the North Atlantic Ocean in the early morning hours of April 15, 1912 after striking an iceberg during her maiden voyage from Southampton to New York City, but **not without warning**!

An ice warning message arrived on the HMS Titanic to the operator Phillips as he worked sending passenger messages. Phillips placed that 'message' in a folder, "to be delivered later" and told the *Californian* operator to stop sending subsequent messages regarding the icebergs: *"Shut up. Shut up. I am busy. I am working Cape Race."* But Phillips never touched that original note that he 'filed', and that critical warning message was never delivered to the Captain or to the bridge. Evans, the original sender of the critical message from the Californian vessel, was less than an hour away from the Titanic. After receiving Phillips' message to stop sending messages, he turned off his wireless and went to bed. The Californian, due to the icebergs, stopped for the night. Therefore, later when Phillips, sent messages requesting S.O.S. help, that could have saved many lives, the messages were not received by the Californian in time for them to rescue any of the Titanic passengers. (from Wikipedia)

Passenger Eye Witness

Edith Russell recalled, "at first nobody took the incident seriously. There were snowball fights from the ice on the deck from the iceberg between passengers." Edith, herself, carefully locked up her valuables in her room and then reluctantly made her way to the lifeboats wearing just a tight sheath dress and velvet pumps as she carried her toy pig to safety. (BBC Archive Broadcast April 14, 1970)

Pastor Onboard

John Harpe, a Pastor and widower with his six-year old daughter, were passengers on the Titanic. Harper was travelling to the Moody Church in Chicago, named for famous founder Dwight L. Moody. The Church was anxiously awaiting his arrival. Harper planned to accept their invitation to be their new Pastor. Harper had been a pastor in two churches, first in Glasgow and then later in London. His was an evangelist, as attested to by another local pastor. "*He was a great open-air preacher and could always command large and appreciative audiences. ... He could deal with all kinds of interrupters, his great and intelligent grasp of Bible truths enabling him to successfully combat all assailants.*" His past had well prepared him for his own 'for such a time as this' moment.

When the Titanic hit the iceberg, Harper successfully led his daughter to a lifeboat. As a widower, he may have been allowed to join her but instead, he chose to forsake his own rescue in an effort to be able to help others. As the water began to submerge the "unsinkable" Titanic, Harper worked to help and encourage passengers to pray and have faith. That led to a strong rebuttal by a man who refused to be encouraged to have faith or assurance of heaven. He rebuked Harper for the message.

Harper then handed the man his own life vest, saying, **"You need this more than I do."** Harper's faith had assured him of his own eternal life through Christ. Harper, until the last moment on the ship, continued to plead with people to trust their lives to Jesus. (Baptist Press, Douglas W. Mize, posted Friday, April 13, 2012**).**

As the HMS Titanic began to sink, the ship band set up on the deck and played, *"Nearer My God to Thee"*. They played this song for as long as they could stand on the deck. The 'unsinkable' Titanic took 1500 passengers, including most of the crew, and all of its 'earthly treasures' on board to the bottom of the ocean on April 15, 1912. But God, in all of this, HAD provided opportunities and warnings that, had the warnings been heeded, would have changed the outcome of this tragedy. God had also provided passengers with the message of eternal life and salvation through Pastor and Evangelist Harper who dutifully prayed with as many as he could during the last moments of their lives.

The Twin Towers -New York City

The twin towers represented the power of New York City and the economic vigor of the United States. The declaration made by the architect at their completion was:

"a living representation of man's belief in humanity, his need for individual dignity, his beliefs in the cooperation of men, and through cooperation, his ability to find greatness."

Minoru Yamasaki, World Trade Center, April 4, 1973

Those who witnessed the events of September 11, 2011 remember exactly where they were and what they were doing when the first highjacked plane hit the first Tower. Hours of terror followed, which included a second highjacked plane hitting the second Tower, and a third highjacked plane crashing into the Pentagon. The fourth highjacked plane has passengers who worked together and were able to retake the plane and divert it from hitting the White House. That plane crashed in a field in PA. There is no way of knowing if other planes were highjacked because all other flights were terminated from flying. The United States President George Bush, Jr. also ordered all government buildings, including the state department, the Capitol building and the White House, be evacuated. Nine top leaders of the House and Senate were taken into federal protection. Other public buildings across the country were evacuated and other evacuations followed: the Washington Monument, the Statue of Liberty, the St Louis Gateway Arch, and Disneyworld in Orlando, all closed their doors. Because of quick actions and people working together, lives were saved.

A Divine Connection

Many of the buildings surrounding the Twin Towers were destroyed and damaged. One notable building that survived was St. Paul's Chapel, located across the street from the World Trade Center. Rabbi Johnathan Cahn was amazed. He began to research the origin of that Chapel building. He discovered that in 1789, in that very Chapel, George Washington held a dedication service for America with other leaders during his inauguration. He discovered that America's first government of "In God We Trust" actually began from that very chapel in New York City long before the government was moved to the District of Columbia.

Rabbi Johnathan Cahn explained in his book "The Harbinger" an uncanny parallel between the 9/11 attack with events in the 8th century with Israel. There was a Bible verse used to dedicate the rebuilding of the site: "The bricks are fallen down, but we will build with hewn stones: the sycamores are cut down, but we will change *them into* cedars" (Isaiah 9:10). This is the very verse that Israel recorded when they went to rebuild in the 8th century. At that time, the nation of Israel was under the judgement of God. The nation of Israel had refused to listen to their prophets and turn back in obedience to God to following and trusting in God, and declared they would rebuild with their strength.

Israel and America are the only nations that sovereignly declared and committed to bring "light" through faith in the Bible, to the world. Those who laid America's foundations, envisioned America as being similar to Israel, and committed America to bring 'light' to the New World.

The nation of Israel strayed from their covenant with God. Rabbi Cahn noted that America, too, like Israel, has departed from its faith in God. The action of removing prayer from the schools, as well as removing the Ten commandments from public areas has opened another door.

Rabbi Jonathan Cahn says before God judges, He sends warning. God sent warnings to ancient Israel, and Cahn believes that the attacks of 9/11 were a warning to America. Cahn is a Jewish messenger to America, declaring that if America, like ancient Israel, ignores God's warning similar consequences to America will follow. Cahn has provided nine harbingers of what happens when a nation refuses to return to God. The judgments are progressive, with periods of normalcy in-between. Judgments continue when there is no national repentance.

HMS Titanic and 9/11

Those who watched the sinking of the Titanic were dramatized by what they witnessed. Those who witnessed the Titanic sinking in 1912, found it to be just as unbelievable as we who witnessed the New York City Twin Towers collapsing and cascading into the ground.

Both events contain man's inability at some point to change earthly outcomes once events are set into place.
Both incidents created an awareness of unexpected physical death.
Both incidents included survivors who lived through the tragedies.
Both forever changed the way we view our world.
Both brought an awareness of the brevity of life.
Both caused many people to ponder the meaning of life, and to value the promises of eternal life contained within the Bible.

Christian Witnesses:
HMS Titanic: John Harper (29 May 1872 – 15 April 1912) was prepared to act courageously during the crisis. He had personally embraced his parents' Christian faith at age 14 and he began preaching at 18. In 1897, he became the first pastor of Paisley Road Baptist Church in Glasgow, Scotland. During the sinking of the HMS Titanic, Harper exercised his faith when he remained on board to help others and to share the message of eternal life with those on board. He was one of those who jumped into the water with others as the ship began to sink. While in the water, he continued to swim to people to tell them to, "Believe on the Lord Jesus Christ, and thou shalt be saved, and thy house" (**Acts 16:31**). Harper was

one of those found dead floating in the water. Harper used his faith to encourage others right until he went home to heaven! His 'for such a time as this' moment reflected the fruit of the Holy Spirit in the midst of extreme fear. He exhibited God's love, care and concern to others.

The Trade Towers – 20 FT Cross:

Following the terrorist attacks, a massive operation was launched to clear the site and attempt to find any survivors amongst the rubble. On September 13, 2001, a worker at the site named Frank Silecchia discovered a 20-foot cross of two steel beams amongst the debris. He, too, had stepped into his own 'for such a time as this' moment providing a ray of hope of eternal life for those who perished that day.

Father Jordan was asked to speak about the steel beamed cross and declared it to be a "symbol of hope, a symbol of faith, a symbol of healing". One minister at the site stated that a man whose family had died had come to stand beside that steel cross. He later said, *"It was as if the cross took in the grief and loss. I never felt Jesus more."*

Faith is a Choice

The Bible says, "God is our refuge and strength, an ever-present help in trouble. Therefore, will not we fear, though the earth be removed, and though the mountains be carried into the midst of the sea, though the waters thereof roar and be troubled, though the mountains shake with the swelling thereof" (Psalm 46: 1-3).

These events are sharp reminders for all of us. NONE of us know when we will be called to exercise our own faith and concern for others within our own 'in such a time as this" moment. What we currently have is 'time' to prepare ourselves as we live out our days on earth. This book is to empower and inspire us to be ready to live for God 'in such a time as this."

COVID19

The Corona Virus known as COVID19 began in early December 2019 in China. Governments around the world shut down businesses, and required people to stay at home. International travel was stopped. People were encouraged not to travel, and to do a 14-day quarantine after travelling, to wear masks and gloves in order to reduce the likely of being infected. The economic impact of business shutdowns will be felt for years to come. Researchers continue to work to understand and to implement strategies to prevent further outbreaks as people mingle again in public.

This event has created worldwide anxiety and fear. Reopening any regular business was met with protestors. Some demanded workers be allowed to go back to work to prevent economic collapse wherever possible, and the others protested to continue the business shut downs in order to prevent deaths. The impact of the virus will be around for years to come.

Why does God allow these things to occur?
Billy Graham said, *"I have been asked hundreds of times why God allows tragedy and suffering. I have to confess that I do not know the answer. I have to accept, by faith, that God is sovereign, and that He is a God of love and mercy and compassion in the midst of suffering."*

Events like the Titantic and the Twin Towers, and now COVID19, provide the world with 'moments' to stop. And while being stopped, there is contained 'a moment' the chance for us to evaluate our entire life's purpose: a chance for us to turn to God, to choose to have faith.

After the towers fell, members of our Congress stood shoulder to shoulder and sang, "God Bless America."

Jesus confirmed that we live in a world filled with suffering. His promise includes assurance of eternal life. "These things I have spoken unto you, that in me ye might have peace. **In the world ye shall have tribulation: but be of good cheer; I have overcome the world**" (John 16:33).

Although no suffering is desired on this earth, the Bible assures us of 'eternal life' for those who choose to believe, where every tear will be someday wiped away.

"And God shall wipe away all tears from their eyes; and there shall be no more death, neither sorrow, nor crying, neither shall there be any more pain: for the former things are passed away" (Revelation 21:4).

"For I reckon that the sufferings of this present time are not worthy to be compared with the glory which shall be revealed in us" (Romans 8:18).

"How Firm a Foundation"
Fear not, I am with thee; O be not dismayed,
For I am thy God, and will give thee aid;
I'll strengthen thee, help thee, and cause thee to stand,
Upheld by my righteous, omnipotent hand.

Christian hymn, published in 1787

Events like the Titanic, 9/11, and COVID 19, as well as natural disasters actually provide us with 'open doors' for great opportunities. Opportunities to turn to God, and have faith in the God of the Bible, and His Son Jesus Christ's work on the cross to provide eternal security and forgiveness for each of us forever. Each day we have opportunities to share our faith with those we love and encourage them to believe as well.

Heaven on Earth - Here and Now?

What many are unaware of, is that there is a current push occurring to create 'heaven on earth' using the scientific knowledge that is available along with technological advances for the world. The solution for mankind seems to appear to be **the** need for a one world government, a one world religion and a one world monetary system. This new system is implementable because of computers and soon and very soon, we will be offered a 'chip' either in our hand or in our forehead that will be required by everyone in order to buy or sell. The solution is to link computer technology within our physical bodies, to enable us instant knowledge for whatever situation we face, instant solutions beyond our ability to calculate and to help us to know what to do, from a computer – instantly. This does sound GREAT! What could possibly be wrong with this plan?

Can we know the future?

Would it surprise you to learn that the Bible contains prophecies that outline exactly what will occur on earth before the return of Jesus Christ to the earth to set up His Kingdom? Yes, prophecies, which include an incredible person who will come and present himself and who will be embraced by the entire world. This wonderful man will be proclaimed by another to be the promised return of the highly anticipated 'Messiah'. But the reality will actually be that this wonderful man will deceive the entire world. His wisdom and knowledge and wonderful solutions for bringing peace to earth for all mankind, will include miracles, signs and wonders. Technology promises to even provide the end of 'death' itself.

The Push for Human Perfection

In the early 20th century, eugenics mania swept America with laws passed in 27 states which forced sterilizations. Scientists and social reformers embraced this approach as the scientific answer to better society in order to breed a better race. Many believe this is the only solution for mankind. The PBS film, "The Eugenics Crusade" by Michelle Ferrari features Adolf Hitler. Hitler, who was inspired by America's sterilization program, used his own program to exterminate the Jews. The same issues exist today that existed then: inequality, urban squalor, tensions over immigration, fear and divisions.

The Technological Singularity

A technological **singularity** will occur when technological growth becomes uncontrollable and irreversible, resulting in unforeseeable changes to human civilization. The intelligence explosion will bring with it a self-improvement cycle, resulting in super intelligence that will surpass human intelligence. This superintelligence will continue to expand technologically at an incomprehensible rate. The singularity point is projected for 2030, or before. Stephen Hawking and Elon Musk have warned that Artificial Intelligence (AI) could cause human extinction as we know it.

Natasha Vita-More is for life extension and proposes the use of scientific and technological advances to allow humans to become whatever they want to be: cat like, or super runners by using he DNA of animals; genes of a leopard, or whatever animal chosen. Genes extracted from animals and implanted within humans provide the opportunity for bodily human enhancements.

James J. Hughes Executive Director of the Institute for Ethics and Emerging Technologies works to enhance human life on earth. Featured in the film 'Inhuman" by Dr. Tom Horn, he asserts that by giving an animal human parts, what should follow is the logical question of whether those animals that have human parts, be considered as 'human'. If human, they therefore should be endowed with human rights.

Dr. Tom Horn's concern is that by creating a new race of genetically enhanced humans, these enhanced humans would be deemed to be superior in nature to those who are born human and who choose not to receive enhancements. Those people could then be viewed as a burden to society and in need of termination for the betterment of the world. This would include all those who refuse to receive a 'computer chip implant' within their physical body.

Natasha Vita-More gives assurance that no one will be forced to take an 'implant' but those who choose to 'not' have implants will be left behind. The 'holy grail' goal of science is to create 'eternal life' for humans who live on earth, right now, so that humans do not die. Heaven on earth, right here and now, with no need for God. Dr. Horn asks, "Will this become the fulfillment of Revelation 9:6? "**And** in those days **shall men seek death, and shall not find it; and shall** desire to die, **and death shall** flee from them."

Opportunities Now:

Our world desperately needs spiritual renewal. We have been given a promise by the Lord who spoke to Solomon:

"And the Lord appeared to Solomon by night, and said unto him, I have heard thy prayer, and have chosen this place to myself for a house of sacrifice. If I shut up heaven that there be no rain, or if I command the locusts to devour the land, or if I send pestilence among my people;

If <u>my people</u>, which are called by my name, shall humble themselves, and pray, and seek my face, and turn from their wicked ways; then will I hear from heaven, and will forgive their sin, and will heal their land" (2 Chronicles 7:12-14).

We are given the amazing promise by the Lord Jesus Christ, "God so loved the world that He gave His only begotten Son, that whoever believes in Him should not perish but have everlasting life. For God sent not his Son into the world to condemn the world; but that the world through him might be saved" (John 3:16-17).

God's promise to believers is 'eternal life' after this life on earth. The Bible predicts the return of the Lord in the air for believers before a seven-year period called, 'the time of Jacob's trouble'. After that terrible time, then Jesus Christ will return to the Mount of Olives to bring peace, love and joy with His reign of one thousand years on earth. After the thousand years, all those on earth will again be provided the opportunity to make their 'free will choice' to have faith and believe in God, or to choose to live life without God. God's goal is to not have programmed 'robots" but to allow us to exercise our free will choice, even if that includes our choice to walk away from His love.

In this lifetime, we have the opportunity to acquire faith, as well as implement our faith in our daily circumstances through prayer and fasting; with our thanks and praise. The test of 'real' faith happens daily.

The Question: The question is will we be able to say as Job did when he experienced loss of his family, wealth and health, "*Naked* came I out of my mother's womb, and **naked shall** I return thither: the LORD gave, and the LORD hath taken away; blessed be the.name of the Lord" (Job 1:21).

God Works all for His Divine Purpose:

God is Good! God is Love! God is Truth! The Creator of all has chosen to allow 'evil' to exist for a specified time on earth. His promise is that he will work all 'evil' for 'good' – if not in this life, in eternity which is forever. We each have a 'choice'. In faith, to believe His promises or to lean unto our own understanding. The information explosion and technological advancements promise to produce 'heaven on earth! FREEDOM to be free from 'faith' itself. This leads us to the question that Jesus asked his disciples while on earth: Jesus asked, "Nevertheless when the Son of man cometh, **shall** he **find faith** on the **earth**?" (Luke 18:8).

Tolerance?

The world talks of 'tolerance'. Unfortunately, the tolerance spoken of includes everything except for tolerance of free speech, or for certain expressions of faith, in particular of faith in Jesus Christ. We may have faith in ourselves, faith in humanity, faith in any religion as long as we do not believe that the Lord Jesus Christ is who He proclaimed Himself to be – the Son of God who came to earth to provide all human beings with eternal life. This has been sanctioned as being 'hate' speech.

"Neither is there salvation in any other: for there is none other name under heaven given among men, whereby we must be saved" (Acts 4:12).

"For if by one mans' offence (Adam's) death reigned by one; much more they which receive abundance of grace and of the gift of righteousness shall reign to life by one, Jesus Christ. Therefore, as by the 'offence of one judgment came upon all men to condemnation; even so by the righteousness of one the free gift came upon all men unto justification of life. For as by one man's disobedience many were made sinners, so by the obedience of one shall many be made righteous" (Romans 5:17-19).

"Eye hath not seen, nor ear heard neither have entered into the heart of man, the things which God hath prepared for them that love him"
(1 Corinthians 2:9).

PRAYER: *Lord help us to value those things that you value, to value life more than material objects. Give us a love for you as Creator, and faith in your written Words. Faith for eternal life, beyond this lifetime.*

For Such a Time as This?

Chapter 2

Intervene, Intervene, Intervene

Ye have not chosen me, but I have chosen you, and ordained you, that ye should go and bring forth fruit, and that your fruit should remain.

John 15:16

"The issue is that we are willingly abject slaves of what is called 'amusement' and 'entertainment' entirely engrossed with every distraction of this world with no will to leave."

Charles Spurgeon, Flowers page 233

God's Intervention

The story is told of a man who went for a trek to find himself, and ended up finding himself in a desert. He had drunk all the water he brought, but noticed something like an oasis ahead of him. There he found a well. At first, he was overjoyed, but quickly dismayed. He was overjoyed when he saw the well, because of the prospect of drinking as much water as he could. Dismayed, because as he looked into the well, he could see there was no 'water' inside the well. Then he noticed a box with a lid on it next to the well. When he opened the box, he found a 'Note". The Note read, "Dig through the sand in this box and you will find a bottle full of water. When you get the bottle of water, DO NOT DRINK IT. Take the water and pour all the water in the bottle into the valve in the handle of the pump for the well. Then once all the water is gone, begin to pump the handle vigorously. As you do so, water will begin to come out of the spot. Fill all the empty bottles you are carrying with water and drink as much as you wish and rest here. When you are revived, be sure to 'refill' the original bottle that you found in this box, and bury that bottle back in the sand, and carefully place this note again on top of the sand for the next weary traveler who comes this way. Again, DO NOT DRINK THE WATER IN THIS BOTTLE. You will be tempted to drink it, to doubt this note, and to believe that if you pour the water out, the pump will not work and you will be left with NOTHING. If you drink the water, you will have no water left to prime the well, and none to fill your bottles, and IF you FORGET to refill this bottle and don't return it under the sand, no one who stops here after you to this place will have access to drinking water after you leave! The reality is our life experience is much like Desert Joe. We take off expecting all to go well, all by ourselves looking for satisfaction from this life, and then are surprised when bad things happen. This makes it harder for us to choose to rely on God to meet our needs when we face a trial, and harder still to pray when there seems to be no way. When God intervenes for us and provides a way out, we must choose to make the sacrifice required of us so that others after us, are empowered to have the same 'water' of life that has been made available to us from God's Holy Spirit. Living for just the joys of this temporary life without regard for God, belief in God, or desire to know God, is hollow and cannot deliver to us the satisfaction that we expect. Such living always leaves us wanting for more, for the next great vacation, the next adventure. Some live simply going from one 'distraction' to another, in an endless attempt to fill that inner longing for 'more' but always ending up needing more still. This is because unless the Lord 'intervenes' we will not seek a relationship with God that is apart from 'earthly things.

"All we like sheep have gone astray; we have turned everyone to his own way" (Isaiah 53:6).

Jesus used a parable of a lost 'sheep' in need of a Shepherd, to convey our need for a relationship with God:

"How think ye? if a man have an hundred sheep, and one of them be gone astray, doth he not leave the ninety and nine, and goeth into the mountains, and seeketh that which is gone astray?[3] And if so be that he find it, verily I say unto you, he rejoiceth more of that sheep, than of the ninety and nine which went not astray. Even so, it is not the will of your Father which is in heaven, that one of these little ones should perish" (Matthew 18:12-14).

In the book "A Shepherd's Look at Psalm 23" W. Phillip Keller gives accounts of his care for sheep in Vancouver Canada. In his book, he reveals that Lost sheep do not know they are lost. If they fall over onto their backs, there is only a very short window available to find them before they die. Sheep tend to follow. One wandering sheep, can lead a whole flock into unprotected areas.

Those of us who love the Lord are asked to intervene not only in prayer but in tangible ways. We are asked to be sure to leave 'water' behind for those who are taken 'captive' by the prince of this world, who uses the lust of the flesh, the lust of the eye, the pride of life and the love of this world to lure us away from living for God. The temptations can also include the misuse of drugs, food, and of alcohol. These excessive focuses can have negative results that impact not only families, and children but entire communities. Everyone knows of families dealing with heartbreaking issues.

The core issue stems from a desire to acquire: "Happiness without 'holiness', and 'pleasure' apart from being pleasing to God."' Charles Spurgeon

God assures us, that as we go to Him and seek His face, read His word and go to Him with our prayers, needs and requests, that He will meet us and give us the joy and peace that we seek. The pattern is:

Believe, pray, wait and then act.

The mystery of faith, which is not according to our own understanding, is a pure conscience. A conscience that when aware of any ill, seeks to make restitution whenever possible. This is the life that is able to overcome evil with good. This is the life that is able to have 'the peace of God' even in the midst of struggles, trials and sufferings.

It is through the power of God's Holy Spirit through answered prayers that that the Lord draws us to Himself. We are much like Mr. Keller's sheep. We need a Shepherd for our eternal soul who seeks and find us when we go astray.

"I pray may love abound yet more and more in knowledge and in all judgment that we may approve things that are excellent that I may be sincere and without offense, filled with the fruits of righteousness which are by Jesus Christ unto the glory and praise of God" (Philippians 1:9-11).

Lord, INTERVENE, INTERVENE, INTERVENE, help us to:
FIGHT THE GOOD FIGHT

Fight the good fight with all thy might

Christ is thy strength And Christ thy 'Right"

Faint not nor fear For His is near

He changeth not and thou art dear.

Only believe and thou shalt see, That Christ is all in all to Thee.

John S.B. Monsell 1811-1873

PRAYER:

Lord, have mercy on us! Intervene and help us! Send your Holy Spirit and empower us as believers with a vision of what needs to be done and empower us with your strength to do those very things. Send your Holy Spirit to open eyes and unstop ears, and help us to walk in faith in what is not seen. We are here on earth for such a short time, yet we act like 'right now' is all that matters. Lord, we are truly helpless and lost without your precious Holy Spirit's guidance and intervention in answer to prayer. Help us to yield to you, and obey your leading moment by moment, This is not "our" will be done, but rather an earnest heartfelt begging for YOU to intervene for Your Name's Sake in answer to this Prayer. Help us to "let go' and 'trust YOU to work on our behalf. Please show us Your way!

Chapter 3

Deliver, Deliver, Deliver

Faithful is he that has called you, who also will do it.

1 Thessalonians 5:24

"For all that is in the world, **the lust of the flesh,** and **the lust of the eyes,** and **the pride of life,** is not of the Father, but **is of the world**" (1 John 2:16).

The Lord Jesus Christ paid a price to **deliver** us in actuality from the lust of the flesh, the lust of the eyes, and the pride of life through the indwelling of His Holy Spirit. Franklin Graham said regarding COVID19, "This outbreak has stripped away many of the idols that we have accumulated in our culture: sports, entertainment, wealth and a false sense of earthy security. As horrific as this pandemic has been, and the staggering toll it has taken on the world, there is a much more horrible disease that has infected mankind – sin. All of us are born as sinners, and that sin has separated us from a holy God."

The message of the Bible is that "God so loved the world that He gave His only begotten son that whosoever (place your name here) believeth on Him shall be saved. For God sent not his Son into the world to condemn the world, but that the world through Him might be saved. He that believeth on him is not condemned, but he that believeth not is condemned already, because he hath not believed in the name of the only begotten Son of God" (John 3:16-17).

Discernment

We are bombarded by media advertisements and commercials that offer products with images that promise to meet our needs as well as fulfill our deep inner desire for recognition, respect and success. We were created to have fellowship with God! The things of this world are here to serve us, NOT for us to serve them. What does this mean? It means that what we own, what we wear, and what we look like, have nothing to do with our real worth. Spiritual connection to God through the work of Jesus Christ on the cross, is possible when God's Holy Spirit is invited within our hearts to live within us. This relationship has eternal value, beyond power, success, and material possessions. Our 'identity' ultimately comes from God who created all things.

Inside NOT Outside

Jesus commended John the Baptist, who was sent as a type of Elijah, to prepare the way for His ministry. Jesus said, "But what went ye out for to see? A man clothed in soft raiment? behold, they that wear soft *clothing* are in kings' houses." But what went ye out for to see? A prophet? Yea, I say unto you, and more than a prophet" (Matthew 11:7-8).

John the Baptist was: "The voice of one crying in the wilderness, prepare ye the way of the LORD, make straight in the desert a highway for our God. Every valley shall be exalted, and every mountain and hill shall be made low: and the crooked shall be made straight, and the rough places plain: And the glory of the LORD shall be revealed, and all flesh shall see it together: for the mouth of the LORD hath spoken it" (Isaiah 43:5).

John the Baptist was put in prison by Herod for declaring it was not lawful for him to be with his brother's wife, John's mission was not to please people, but rather to proclaim the truth to those who would listen, to speak of the acceptable time of the Lord. There are connections between the physical world and the spiritual world on every level. Deliverance can occur from just our ordinary oversights and actions as well.

Spared

Being 'spared' the pain from the consequences of our actions is a wonderful thing. Sometimes we are spared, but there is no way of knowing that we were spared. Other times, we clearly can see that our unexpected delay in leaving on a trip, caused us to end up behind an accident on the highway that occurred just ahead of us, and we realize 'that small delay' saved us from being in that accident ourselves. Occasionally, the Lord allows us to see when we were spared. Recently, I filled my arms with things to deliver to others. Then I proceeded to the garage, opened the garage door, loaded the car, got in, started the car and began to back up, when I saw my husband Fabien enter the garage and wave his arms in the air, wildly. I braked and rolled down my window to ask what was up. He looked relieved and exclaimed, 'Look behind you!" I looked in my car rear view mirror and was shocked to see the garage door had closed. I was less than an inch from going right through the 'closed' door. I shut the car off and got out and went and gave Fabien a hug. He told me, "I was sure I was going to watch you back right into that door!" I said, "I am so relieved you were able to stop me! Whatever caused you to come into the garage at that very moment?" He replied, "I have no idea!" We hugged. He said, "I am so glad we won't have to add new garage doors this year!" I had been spared! We both knew that it was the leading of God's Holy Spirit that caused him to come at the exact moment necessary to deliver me from consequences of an action.

We are commanded:

"Love not the world, neither the things that are in the world. If any man love the world, the love of the Father is not in him. And the world passeth away, and the lust thereof: but he that doeth the will of God abideth forever" (1 John 2:15-17).

Let us "walk worthy, of the vocation wherewith ye are called, with all lowliness and meekness with longsuffering forbearing one another in love" (Ephesians 4:2).

PRAYER:

*Lord **deliver us** and keep us from the snares of this world and give us discernment and help us to make sound judgements moment by moment in obedience to your Holy Spirit's guidance according to your will.*

Chapter 4

Recover, Recover, Recover

It is of the Lord's mercies that we are not consumed because His compassions fail not, they are new every morning, great is His faithfulness.

Lamentations 3:22-23

Our 'Faith' is allowed to be tried during 'times of adversity' that contain great losses, sorrow and pain. Life's trials arrive unexpectedly without warning; often when things are going well. Once a trial starts, we think 'things' just can't get worse! But often when things are at their worst, more bad news arrives. It is when we reach 'bottom' that we are more open to seek God for help. "Hitting bottom" we have zero strength to continue. Depression sets in, and discouragement follows. Thoughts of 'just ending life' can arrive, along with questions, "Where is God? Why did **this** have to happen?"

"Job" in the Bible lost his family, his wealth, and his health, all within a very short period of time. This account includes the answer to why God allow suffering. God blessed Job abundantly with wealth, health and family. Job "was perfect and upright, and one that feared God, and eschewed evil" (Job 1:1). God placed a hedge of protection around Job from Satan.

The account of Job's life begins with a conversation in heaven between God and Satan about the faithfulness of Job. Satan accuses Job of being faithful to God only for health and wealth. One day in heaven there was a meeting, Satan came also, and Satan challenged God, "Put forth thine hand now, and touch all that he hath, and he will curse thee to thy face" (Job 1:11). The Lord said, "Behold, all that he hath is in thy power, only upon himself put not forth thine hand" (Job 1:12).

God's hedge of protection was removed! Satan took action, "And there was a 'day"(Job 1:13-14). When the dust settled, Job had lost oxen, asses, servants, sheep, camels, sons and daughters, and his house, in that order. In his distress Job shouted, "Naked I came out of my mother's womb, and naked shall I return thither, the Lord gave, and the Lord hath taken away; blessed be the name of the Lord" (Job 1:21-22). When Job did not curse God, Satan challenged God again, "Put forth thine hand now, and touch his bone and his flesh, and he will curse you to thy face" (Job 2:5). God permitted a further refinement of Job. "Behold he is thine hand: but save his life" (Job 2:6). Satan, "smote Job with sore boils from the sole of his foot unto his crown" (Job 2:7). This was more than Job's wife could handle and she exclaimed, "Curse God, and die" (Job 2:9). But Job responded, "What? Shall we receive good at the hand of God, and shall we not receive evil? In all this did not Job sin with his lips" (Job 2:10).

Trouble and sorrow are allowed in this world because Lucifer, the fallen angel, now called "Satan" who was cast down to the earth, is allowed to test men on earth. He is "going to and for in the earth, and from walking up and down in it" (Job 2:2). "Be sober, be vigilant; because your adversary the devil, as a roaring lion, walketh about, seeking whom he may devour: Whom resist stedfast in the faith, knowing that the same afflictions are accomplished in your brethren that are in the world" (1 Peter 5:8).

The Lord's instructions are:

"Therefore whosoever heareth these sayings of mine, and doeth them, I will liken him unto a wise man, which built his house upon a rock: And the rain descended, and the floods came, and the winds blew, and beat upon that house; and it fell not: for it was founded upon a rock.

And every one that heareth these sayings of mine, and doeth them not, shall be likened unto a foolish man, which built his house upon the sand: And the rain descended, and the floods came, and the winds blew, and beat upon that house; and it fell: and great was the fall of it" (Matthew 7:24-27).

My own hiding place during trials is to imagine myself being the size of a grain of sand. I then place 'myself' within the nail hole of the Savior's hand. I remain there within my mind's eye, and remind myself of God's promises. "Let thy mercies come also unto me, O Lord, even my salvation according to Thy word" (Psalm 119:41).

We are assured that life will bring us face to face with mountains of fear, doubt, and disbelief. How can we deal with sorrow and loss? What can we do to help us move forward? Answers to those questions are provided through God's promises within the Holy Scriptures of the Bible.

King Saul was a tormented soul, challenged to walk in faith. He learned of a lad who sang and played the harp. David the shepherd boy, was summoned to King Saul's tent. David's singing was able to calm Saul's heart and mind. Hymns can lift our spirit and calm us as well.

David himself experienced unexpected trials, after huge victories. David was not a stranger to trouble, loss, sorrow and loneliness. He wrote most of the Psalms. One of David's songs, proclaims: "My soul **MELTED** for **HEAVINESS** strengthen thou me according to thy word" (Psalm 119:28). 'Melting' is caused by extreme heat, and this is the "word' that David used to describe the intensity of his loss, sorrow and pain. Such intensity drains any strength we have and leaves us empty and bereft.

My own desire is always to 'RUN' to get away from pain. I have learned running solves nothing. The only place for us to "RUN' *is to the Lord* in prayer with tears, pleas, on knees! David exclaimed, "I will **RUN** the way of thy commandments when thou shalt enlarge my heart" (Psalm 119:32).

God Will Take Care of You
David Phelps

You don't say a word, but I know you're suffering
Trying hard to take a step of Faith.
You're so confused and you're so alone
Standing face to face with the unknown.
Every need you have God already knows about it
Still he longs to hear from you.
I believe, if you put your trust in Him
That is where the road of faith begins.

If His eye is on the sparrow, when it comes to me and you
There is no place He won't go, and nothing He won't do
Like a mother cradle's a child, His grace covers us somehow
So, whatever you go through, God will take care of you!

Change is never easy but it is part of living. There's so much more than what we can see. A higher place, so far above it all, is ours when we're faithful to his Call. Cause, if his eye is on the sparrow, when it comes to me and you, there is no place He won't go and nothing he won't do.
You don't have to know: the how's the why's the where's, so give it all to Him. God WILL take care of you!
You'll be all right, because He'll take care of you!

PRAYER:

*Lord, help us to **NOT lean unto our own understanding**. Help us to recognize that our minds are like cups in comparison to the ocean of your love. Help us Lord to remember that we are unable to comprehend within our limited space and time the wonders of 'eternity' which you are preparing for us.*

*Help us to have faith and to believe, even when our world falls apart. Help us to look for and wait for your promise to **'work all for our good'**. Help us to be able to praise you in the midst of sorrow, pain, and loss that is beyond comprehension.*

Help us to trust you and look for the eternal joys that you have promised to all them that love and trust you!

*Lord, **recover us from our unbelief** and help us to just trust that you have a purpose in all that you allow. Help us when we are asked to carry our very own cross, for we know you have gone before us through such pain and sorrow on the cross, and are now alive forever more!*

"Looking unto Jesus the author and finisher of *our* faith; who **for the joy that was set before him endured the cross**, despising the shame, and is set down at the right hand of the throne of God" (Hebrews 12:2).

Thank you for the assurance of eternal life through your Son Jesus Christ.

LORD: "Keep me as the apple of the eye, hide me under the shadow of thy wings" (Psalm 18:8).

For Such a Time as This?

Chapter 5

Redeem, Redeem, Redeem

Be strong and of good courage; be not afraid, neither be thou dismayed, for the Lord thy God is with thee, withersoever thou goest.

Joshua 1:9

The most amazing thing about the Lord is that He loves each of us as though there were only ONE of us.

You can fill in your 'name' with every promise given within the scriptures, because they are written specifically with 'you' in mind.

"Beloved, let us love one another, for love is of God; and everyone that loveth is born of God, and is of God. He that loveth not, knoweth not God, for God is Love" (1 John 4:7-8).

Love is an 'Action" Word

Witnessing 'redemption' in action is quite a sight to see! This happens when something deemed totally worthless has been tossed into a burn pile.

The Chest

When renovations were done to our garage, there was a need for an additional door that could open onto the new extended truck port area. My husband, Fabien began scrolling the postings for a door and located one that was posted by a friend of his. He arranged for us to go and get the door. When we arrived, both of us noticed a large black chest on a burn pile behind his friend's home. His friend was moving and tossing items that were broken. Fabien commented right away, "I wonder what the chest is doing on that burn pile?" I replied, "Well, ask him what's wrong with it." Fabien bought and loaded our newly acquired slightly used entry door, and as he loaded that door, he turned to his friend and casually said, "What's up with that chest?" His friend replied, "It's broken, missing its top! You can have it, if you want it!" Fabien replied, "Well I'll look at it." Both of them went and turned the chest over. I could see from my seat in Fabien's truck there was no top on the chest, it was just a big empty box. Fabien picked it up and loaded it on top of the door in the back of his truck and we headed home. I was NOT very excited that we now had another item that required work, but was glad that Fabien felt that the chest could be fixed. "How?" I did not know. Once home, the chest was unloaded and placed in a corner of the garage. Other tasks required his attention, so the chest remained broken and unusable for over a year. When it came time to clean out our garage, I suggested we bring the chest to Habitat. It was taking up needed space, and likely someone would be able to redeem it, other than Fabien. But Fabien wanted to keep it, so it was spared.

When our new friends Caroline and Adam purchased their new home in Vermont, we invited them to visit our garage to pick items that they might like for their new home. As we sorted things, that chest surfaced yet again, and Caroline and Adam liked it and asked if they could have it. Fabien told them that he would work to add a cover to the chest for them and he began to work on it. Progress was slow. Clearly this was a larger task than Fabien had thought. Daily I would check in to see how things were going with it, and slowly his work was beginning to show progress. One day Fabien asked me, "Can you come and help me to attach the cover to the chest?" We went together, me holding the top while he screwed on the hardware to allow the top to open and close.

Caroline and Adam now use that chest as their living room table, and love it because it allows them to store puzzles, and other things inside.

Redeemed by a vision. God's desire and vision is to redeem each of us. God has done the work for us to be **'redeemed'** Our decisions can bring us to our own 'burn piles' where others deem us to be unredeemable. But the Lord seeks us out! Just as Fabien sought out that chest, went and examined it, and claimed it for his own, so too, God will do the work to redeem us as well! He will then use us for a brand-new purpose that brings Him joy and that gives us new life and purpose! Fanny Crosby wrote many hymns to describe the joy of her salvation. Redeemed is one of my favorites!

REDEEMED HOW I LOVE TO PROCLAIM IT!

Redeemed, how I love to proclaim it!
Redeemed by the blood of the Lamb;
Redeemed through His infinite mercy,
His child and forever I am.

Redeemed, redeemed,
Redeemed by the blood of the Lamb;
Redeemed, redeemed,
His child and forever I am.

Redeemed, and so happy in Jesus,
No language my rapture can tell;
I know that the light of His presence
With me doth continually dwell.

I think of my blessed Redeemer,
I think of Him all the day long:

I sing, for I cannot be silent;
His love is the theme of my song.

I know I shall see in His beauty
The King in whose law I delight;
Who lovingly guardeth my footsteps,
And giveth me songs in the night.

I know there's a crown that is waiting
In yonder bright mansion for me,
And soon, with the spirits made perfect,
At home with the Lord I shall be.

"And they sung a new song, saying, Thou art worthy to take the book, and to open the seals thereof: for thou wast slain, and hast **redeemed** us to God by thy blood out of every kindred, and tongue, and people, and nation" (Revelation 5:9).

PRAYER:

***Lord**, thank you for your love for us, for redeeming us and providing us with a new way of living to bring glory and honor to your Holy Name! Thank you that you do not see as man sees. Praise you that you value us beyond what we look like, what we can do, and what we have achieved. Thank you that you love us because you 'created' us and that your heart's desire is to have fellowship with us through your Holy Spirit.*

Chapter 6

Restore, Restore, Restore

Be strong and of good courage; be not afraid, neither be thou dismayed, for the Lord thy God is with thee, withersoever thou goest.

Joshua 1:9

Faith is NOT by SIGHT! Alas, even King Herod and Pilate became friends after being 'at enmity between themselves" (Luke 23:12). Jesus had been brought before Pilate by the Jews who accused Jesus of 'perverting the nation, and forbidding to give tribute to Caesar, saying that he himself is Christ a King" (Luke 23:2). When Pilate heard Jesus was of Galilee, he sent him to Herod from that jurisdiction to deal with the issue. "Herod was exceeding glad for he was desirous to see him of a long season, because he had heard many things of him and he hoped to have seen some miracle done by him" (Luke 23: 8). When Jesus did not oblige, Herod "arrayed him in a gorgeous robe, and sent him again to Pilate' (Luke 23:11). And the same day Pilate and Herod were made friends together" (Luke 23:12). Herod wanted to **SEE** to have FAITH. And oddly enough there was a sense of joy that occurred between Pilate and Herod, when Herod returned his power to Pilate so he could determine the fate of Jesus! Jesus himself told Pilate, "You would have no power over me were it not given to you from above. Therefore, the one that handed me over to you is guilty of a greater sin" (John 19:11). Judas Iscariot, one of his own disciples, betrayed him with a 'kiss'.

The message of Jesus is of RESTORATION of 'Relationship" with God and with one another through FAITH in God. "Seek ye **FIRST** the Kingdom of

God and His Righteousness and all these things shall be added unto you" (Matthew 6:33).

When we agree to **come to God by FAITH** we are RESTORED to fellowship with God. It is FAITH that creates the bridge for us to cross over from the physical realm into the Spiritual realm where God's Holy Spirit can begin His work within our hearts to solidify our Faith.

Peter learned the lesson of 'walking by faith' and not by sight when he boldly stepped out of the boat to meet the Lord who was walking on water towards the boat. Peter walked on water, but only for a short distance before he looked at the water and began to sink, and cried out to the Lord to save him. Jesus held out his hand and assisted him back to the boat.

Our **restoration** occurs when we are willing to take his 'yoke' upon us, for it is there that we find our true worth and the rest we long for. This is where we exchange our burden for His peace and Joy. This is where the restorative power of His shed blood for us is able to gift to us His Holy Spirit's Power and might!

"Come unto me all ye who are weary and heavy laden and I will give thee rest. Take my yoke upon you and ye shall find rest for your souls, for my hoke is easy and my burden is light" (Matthew 11:28-30).

Be Thou My Vision (Irish Hymn)

Be Thou my vision, oh Lord of my heart
Naught be all else to me, save that Thou art
Thou my best thought by day or by night
Waking or sleeping Thy, presence my light

Be Thou my wisdom and Thou my true word
I ever with Thee and Thou with me, Lord

Thou my great Father and I Thy true son
Thou in me dwelling and I with Thee one

Riches I heed not, nor man's empty praise
Thou mine inheritance, now and always
Thou and Thou only, first in my heart
High King of Heaven, my treasure Thou art

Be Thou my vision, oh Lord of my heart
Naught be all else to me, save that Thou art
Thou my best thought by day or by night
Waking or sleeping Thy, presence my light

High King of Heaven, my victory won
May I reach Heaven's joys, oh bright Heaven's sun
Heart of my own heart, whatever befall
Still be my vision, oh Ruler of all
Still be my vision, oh Ruler of all

"God has not given us a spirit of fear, but of POWER and of LOVE, and of a SOUND MIND" (2 Timothy 1:7).

"Finally, brethren, whatsoever things are true, whatsoever things are honest, whatsoever things are just, whatsoever things are pure, whatsoever things are lovely, whatsoever things are of good report; if there be any virtue, and if there be any praise, think on these things" (Philippians 4:8).

Truth

"I am the way, **the truth**, and the life, no man cometh unto the Father but by me" (John 14:6).

PRAYER:

Help me to be yielded 'by my own choice' to you Lord today, a 'vessel' for your use. Give me discernment, wisdom, and spiritual understanding.

Help me Lord to "Let Go – and Let You be in control".

Help me to pray and to ask and not to be vested in the outcomes. Let my only motive be 'to be a vessel unto Thee". Let me glory in fellowship with Thee more than in life itself! Let me be yielded and obedient to Thy Holy Spirit's leading that "YOUR" will may be done on earth as it is in Heaven – through me, TODAY!

Chapter 7

Spiritual Rest

Come unto me, all ye that labour and are heavy laden, and I will give you rest.

Matthew 11:29

One thing we desire the most is 'rest'. The rest that is offered to us from the Lord, is different than the rest offered by the world.

Each day, imagine 'time' as being contained within an 'hour glass' of sand. At the beginning of each day, all our activities and time are within the upper glass chamber. Each minute and task, await their turn to pass through the narrow middle section to go into the lower glass chamber. Time and tasks are completed within 'moments' of time. For each moment, God is able to give us the physical and mental energy we need for that particular task.

God's power is available to us within each 'task' as we do it, and that very power contains within it a divine rest. A 'rest' that is real because the presence of God's Holy Spirit is actually empowering us physically. This is an amazing 'spiritual rest' - a gift of the presence of His Holy Spirit with us.

A sense of timelessness can actually occur that makes time seem to stop or 'stand still'. We have worked for hours, but feel as though only minutes have passed.

Traveling with the Lord is possible:

"My presence shall go with thee, and I will give thee rest" (Exodus 33:14).

The requirement for God's Spiritual Rest:
"Take my yoke upon you, and learn of me; for I am meek and lowly in heart: and ye shall find rest unto your souls" (Matthew 11:29).

The Lord expects us to abide by His program to remain physically strong and well. The Ten Commandments given to Moses were not given to be "optional" or just 'suggestions". The designer of the universe knows 'rest' is what is required for our immune systems to work properly. Even machines need 'down time'.

There is a cost for disregarding the Commandments. The cost may not be felt immediately, but there is an impact on us. When our physical body does not get rest it can be harder to concentrate and we are more likely to be sick.

"Six days thou shalt work, but on the seventh day thou shalt rest: in earing time and in harvest thou shalt rest" (Exodus 34:21).

It is an exercise of faith in God for us to stop and rest, but resting contains a reward of God's strength: "In quietness and in confidence shall be your strength, but ye would not" (Isaiah 30:15). We are 'stubborn' and few are willing to believe that God's day of rest is 'good'.

Jesus, I am Resting, Resting

Jesus! I am resting, resting
In the joy of what Thou art;
I am finding out the greatness
  Of Thy loving heart.
Thou hast bid me gaze upon Thee,
And Thy beauty fills my soul,
For, by Thy transforming power,
  Thou hast made me whole.
Jesus! I am resting, resting
In the joy of what Thou art;
I am finding out the greatness
  Of Thy loving heart
Oh, how great Thy loving kindness,
Vaster, broader than the sea:
Oh, how marvelous Thy goodness,
  Lavished all on me!
Yes, I rest in Thee, Beloved,
Know what wealth of grace is Thine,
Know Thy certainty of promise,
  And have made it mine.
Simply trusting Thee, Lord Jesus,
I behold Thee as Thou art,
And Thy love, so pure, so changeless,
  Satisfies my heart,
Satisfies its deepest longings,
Meets, supplies its every need,
Compassed me round with blessings,
  Thine is love indeed.
Ever lift Thy face upon me,
As I work and wait for Thee;
Resting 'neath Thy smile, Lord Jesus,
  Earth's dark shadows flee.
Brightness of my Father's glory,
Sunshine of my Father's face,
Keep me ever trusting, resting,
  Fill me with Thy grace.

PRAYER:
Lord, this day is so busy. I need your help to navigate through the tasks and to keep and maintain my joy and fellowship with you. Please open 'doors' for me with those that I meet to know how to connect with them. Let me be sensitive to each opportunity and give me the courage that I need to 'go through' sharing your message of love and peace amidst the storms of our lives.

Chapter 8

Pray

"Enter His gates with thanksgiving and courts with praise: be thankful unto him, and bless his name"

(Psalm 100:4).

When we choose to trust God and place our faith in the work of Jesus to forgive us for the wrongs we have done, God saves our eternal soul. I came very close to living a very different life with my own self sufficiency and doing what I believed to be right. It was God who opened a door for me to see that I did indeed need His mercy and forgiveness.

I was 23 years old. I was born into the denomination of my family. I went to church, I was baptized as a baby, I had a first communion, and then did prescribed religious acts. This activity 'inoculated' me into believing all was well, when all was not well. All these outward actions attempt to do something that God has already done for us. "Not by works of righteousness that we have done, but by His mercy He saved us, by the washing and regeneration and renewing of the Holy Ghost which he shed on us abundantly through Jesus Christ our Savior" (Titus 3:5-7).

What a wonderful 'gift' the Lord has provided to ALL through coming to the earth in the form of a baby, living life here as a human, and showing us what 'love' looks like. I challenge you to read the gospels of Matthew, Mark, Luke and John for yourself. Read from your heart the accounts of these four individuals about Jesus Christ, the man of Truth, Love and

Light. Don't worry about what you don't understand, pay attention to what grabs your heart, and then re-read those verses and let them soak into your very being. This is like watering a plant that has soil that is totally dry, the 'water' runs right through the pot. The soil is so 'dry' that it is unable to absorb the water. But place that pot in a solid bowl and let it just soak in water, and the plant will suddenly come alive. We, too, come alive from the living words written for us and preserved by the power of the Lord into eternity.

My questions:

What is your life going to be in the end when you give an account?

What will you have to give to the Lord when you meet him?

Why not choose to give your 'self' to the Lord and ask Him to help you to become a 'vessel' for His use?

Then, have an attitude of GRATITUDE as you begin to be willing and ready to do WHATEVER he has for you to do. Start every day with reading a few chapters from the Bible. Then ask Jesus to help you to make the right decisions. Pray about those things that are happening! Be willing to 'give up' YOUR will to seek HIS will. This is what Jesus meant when he promised us 'life" more abundant! God seeks those who will trust, and walk by FAITH and not by SIGHT. And begin to give glory to God in all that you say, and do. Jesus is calling your name – can you hear Him?

As Jesus was taken up into the air, off the earth He proclaimed, "All power is given unto me in heaven and on earth." He gave the great commission to 'Go' and a reminder "Lo, I am with you always even to the end of the world." (Matthew 28: 18-20)

We have a free gift of salvation through Jesus Christ's sacrifice on our behalf. Make your 'verbal commitment' to Jesus, it is indeed recognized in heaven just as a wedding vow is recognized on earth. And when we call upon His name, seeking His mercy and forgiveness, our names are written in His book of life forever and no 'man' will be able to change our eternal destiny that is sealed by God for eternity.

Our Father which Art in Heaven

Our Father, who art in heaven,
hallowed be thy Name,
thy kingdom come,
thy will be done,
on earth as it is in heaven.

Give us this day our daily bread.
And forgive us our trespasses,
as we forgive those
who trespass against us.

And lead us not into temptation,
but deliver us from evil.
For thine is the kingdom,
and the power, and the glory,
for ever and ever. Amen.

PRAYER:

Lord, we praise you and thank you, for doing all the work for us, and allowing us to just 'come' and learn of you, because your yoke is 'easy' and your burden is 'light'" (Matthew 16: 28-30).

Help me Lord to see what you want me to see, and to do those things that you would have me do – today! Be with those that I love and help them! Help us Lord to have mental clarity, physical health and strength and emotional stability to do what needs to be done today.

Lord, protect us and keep us by the power of your Holy Spirit.

Send you angels to guide, lead and help us,

I ask these things in the precious name of Jesus.

Lord, forgive us, have mercy on us, and help us!

Intervene *with your power for your name's sake, and for the sake of this prayer.*

Deliver *us Lord from the lusts of the flesh, the lusts of the eye, the pride of life and the love of this world.*

Redeem *us through your shed blood and give us fellowship with you.*

Restore *us through your Holy Spirit. Restore our relationships – one with another, and give us your mercy and grace.*

Recover *us from the snares of the enemy who seeks to keep us from the best that you have for us, by diversion and distraction and help us to give you the glory and honor due your Holy Name!*

Chapter 9

Yielded

"But yield yourselves unto God, as those that are alive from the dead, and your members as instruments of righteousness unto God."

Romans 6:13

There are great privileges for those who decide to 'yield' to the Lord's teachings; for those who incorporate within their life the truths contained in the Bible. The world's message is to fill your life with 'things' and 'activities' and enjoy life to its fullest. Those who believe the Bible are deemed to be narrow-minded and wrong.

There are 'mysteries' contained within the 66 books of the Bible that can only be understood by those who become 'yielded' and willing to follow God's Holy Spirit without having to understand everything. There is a reason for that. Jesus disclosed this fact to his disciples when they were alone together. "Unto you it is given to know the mysteries of the kingdom of God: but to others in parables; that seeing they might not see, and hearing they might not understand" (Luke 8:10).

The reason is, once we understand, we are responsible for implementing the truth. Even plants must grow up before they can bear fruit. So, too, believers must grow in knowledge and comprehension in order to be able to withstand the attacks of the devil. We do not allow a child to drive a car. And those who are permitted to drive must pass a Driver Safety Course because accidents can cause instantaneous death.

Likewise, discretion, prayer, and discernment are requirements for sharing faith with others. When we speak to others, it is very important that we respect the free will choice given to them by God. We must be prepared to answer questions and ready to say we don't know. Ready to apologize when we sense offense. Jesus used a parable of sowing seeds to illustrate what happens when people hear the words of the Bible for the first time.

"Now the parable is this: The **seed is the word of God**. Those by **the way side** are they that **hear**; then cometh **the devil, and taketh away the word out of their hearts**, lest they should believe and be saved. They on **the rock** are they, which, when they **hear, receive the word with joy**; and these have **no root**, which for a while believe, and **in time of temptation fall away**. And that which fell **among thorns** are they, which, when they have heard, go forth, and are **choked with cares and riches and pleasures of this life,** and bring no fruit to perfection. But that on the good ground are they, which in an **honest and good heart,** having heard the word, **keep it, and bring forth fruit with patience**" (Luke 8:11-15).

One Way Signs

When Jesus Christ spoke the truth, many walked away. Should we expect anything different? The Lord has promised to continue to draw all men unto himself. The events of life become "One Way Signs" designed to move us closer to faith in God. "Road blocks" require us to turn around, "Free will choice' remains, but we are forced to process different information.

No one chooses to go down a 'Dead End" unless there is a specific reason to do so. Life's unexpected 'outcomes' require us to stop. Deaths, sicknesses, diseases, addictions, crime, bad choices, etc. draw us together to cry, talk and process our sorrow, grief and loss. With grief and sorrow come losses. There are no real answers to the why's of suffering on earth. To have faith we must 'yield' to the wisdom of a Mighty God greater than our own ability to comprehend and understand. And that is a 'choice'. When we exercise our FAITH in the work of the Lord Jesus Christ during this lifetime, we will, in turn, walk down a very strait narrow way.

"Because strait is the gate, and narrow is the way, which leadeth unto life, and few there be that find it" (Matthew 7:14).

Our purpose:

Those who choose to follow the Lord Jesus Christ's teachings, take the strait narrow way and become 'laborers in His Harvest'. Jesus asked us to pray for one another. He asked us to, "Pray ye therefore the Lord of the Harvest, that he would send forth laborers into his harvest" (Matthew 9:38).

Our work: "But sanctify the Lord God in your hearts, and be ready always to give an answer to every man that asketh you a reason of the hope that is in you with meekness and fear" (1 Peter 3:15).

"The greatest worldly advantages cannot compensate for the loss of spiritual privileges." Charles Spurgeon, Flowers pg. 250

Amazing Grace

Amazing grace! how sweet the sound,
  That saved a wretch; like me!
I once was lost, but now am found,
  Was blind, but now I see.

The Lord hath promised good to me,
  His word my hope secures;
He will my shield and portion be
  As long as life endures.

Twas grace that taught my heart to fear,
  And grace my fears relieved;
How precious did that grace appear
  The hour I first believed!

When we've been there ten thousand years,
  Bright shining as the sun,
We've no less days to sing God's praise
  Than when we first begun.

John Newton 1725-1807

PRAYER:

Lord forgive me for my unyieldedness and help me to make it my goal to find my delight in you and your words. Allow those very words to transform my hard, stony heart to become your heart and help me to then see what you would have me to see, and to go where you would have me to go, and to do what you would have me to do. Let me praise you daily in all that I do, think, or say. That you may receive the glory that is due your Holy Name!

Chapter 10

Singlemindedness

If therefore thine eye be single, thy whole body shall be full of light.

Matthew 6:22

The 'meek' not the 'proud' shall inherit the earth (Matthew 5:5).

Jesus had a powerful discussion with a Samaritan woman as he sat on the side of Jacob's well. The woman had come alone to draw water at noon, the hottest time of the day to avoid meeting people. Jesus had stopped at that well, and when he asked her for a drink, she responded with a question. She asked "Why?" Why would he, being a Jew even talk to her? She was a Samaritan! Jews judged Samaritan's for intermarriages with non-Jews! Certainly, being a Jew, he must know that! But Jesus was talking with her, and even with respect! Jesus said, "Go, call thy husband and come hither." The woman answered, "I have no husband". Jesus complimented her, "Thou hast well said, I have no husband, for thou hast had five husbands, and he whom thou now hast is not thy husband: in that saidist thou truly" (John 4:17-18). The woman declared she knew spiritual things as well, proclaiming, "Our Fathers worshipped in this mountain, and ye say, that in Jerusalem is the place where men ought to worship." Jesus responded, "Woman, believe me, the hour cometh, when ye shall neither in this mountain, nor yet at Jerusalem, worship the Father. Ye worship ye know not what, we know what we worship for salvation is of the Jews. But the hour cometh, and now is when the true worshipers shall worship the Father in Spirit and in truth, for the Father seeketh such to worship him. God is Spirit and they that worship Him must worship Him in Spirit and in truth" (John 4:21-24). Hearing these truths, the woman replied, "I know that Messiah cometh, which is called Christ: when he is come, he will tell us all things." Jesus saith unto her, "I that speak unto thee am he." Shocked, this woman left her water pot at the well, and went into the city to tell everyone that she had met the Messiah and she implored them, "come and see a man which told me all things that ever I did, is not this the Christ?" (John 4:28-29).

Truth 'pushes us' out of our daily routine and produces a singlemindedness that is honored by the Lord, who meets us right where we are with His love, compassion and healing. The Lord, in fact, is actually seeking 'us'! He already knows the answers to the questions that he asks. He asks those questions, so that we can 'see' what he sees.

Grady and the Door

My sister Audrey's kitten, Grady, has had a lot of adventures as he discovers and explores the world in which he lives. One of his fascinations is a closed door located at the top of a spiral staircase in our home. My sister resides on the lower level of our home, and Fabien and I reside on the upper level of the home and we have that door between floors. Grady will come and sit at the top of the staircase to look at the light that comes through the bottom of that closed door.

He waits on the top step for the door to open, sometimes for hours with a singlemindedness of purpose, to get to the other side of that door! The first time I found him there, he came running through the door when I opened it. I laughed and laughed. His singlemindedness of purpose had been rewarded!

Us

Like the woman at the well, our encounter with the Lord Jesus Christ in our own life places us on a new path, to seek and understand eternal things. The day Grady got to come through that door, I exclaimed to the Lord, "I am just like Grady, Lord! I, too, see the 'light' from eternity's view, and I long to have fellowship with you, who dwell on the other side. I am blessed to see 'glimpses' of your glory and honor, but someday, like Grady, I will be allowed 'in' to dwell with you forever."

Here and Now: What a privilege it is 'here and now' to have assurance of eternal life while we are on earth! Like the woman, the more we know, the more we want to know. The good news is that we are empowered by the Lord to acquire our own 'singlemindedness' within whatever we are doing. Being focused opens opportunities for us to not only learn and grow, but to be present for those we love to give encouragement and hope, even as Jesus did for the woman at the well.

Someday: "Every man's work shall be made manifest: for the day shall declare it, because it shall be revealed by fire; and the fire shall try every man's work of what sort it is. If any man's work abide which he hath built thereupon, he shall receive a reward. If any man's work shall be burned, he shall suffer loss: but he himself shall be saved; yet so as by fire" (1 Corinthians 3:13-15).

Right now: "I therefore so run, not as uncertainly; so fight I, not as one that beateth the air: But I keep under my body, and bring it into subjection: lest that by any means, when I have preached to others, I myself should be a castaway" (1 Corinthians 9:26-27).

To God be the Glory

To God be the glory, great things He hath done,
So loved He the world that He gave us His Son,
Who yielded His life our redemption to win,
And opened the life-gate that all may go in.
Praise the Lord, praise the Lord,
  Let the earth hear His voice;
Praise the Lord, praise the Lord,
  Let the people rejoice;
Oh, come to the Father, through Jesus the Son,
  And give Him the glory; great things He hath done.
Oh, perfect redemption, the purchase of blood,
To every believer the promise of God;
The vilest offender who truly believes,
That moment from Jesus a pardon receives.
Great things He hath taught us, great things He hath done,
And great our rejoicing through Jesus the Son;
But purer, and higher, and greater will be
Our wonder, our transport when Jesus we see.

Franny Crosby 1820-1915

PRAYER:

Lord help me to recognize how short my time on earth really is and let that awareness empower me to seek you and to be obedient to your leading, that I may abide within our perfect will in my life.

Chapter 11

Be Still

Be still, and know that I am God: I will be exalted among the heathen, I will be exalted in the earth.

Psalm 46:10

It is our 'heart' that the Lord treasures. It is what we 'love' that either unites us to one another, or divides us from others and from God.

"Love not the world, neither the things that are in the world. If any man love the world, the love of the Father is not in him. For all that is in the world, the lust of the flesh, and the lust of the eyes, and the pride of life, is not of the Father, but is of the world. And the world passeth away, and the lust thereof: but he that doeth the will of God abideth for ever" (1 John 2:15-17).

It is when we stop 'doing' and come into the presence of the Lord that we empowered to 'hear' His still small voice. We live in a very 'busy' world. When a 'shelter at home' order was issued due to the Corona Virus around the world, there was within that order the opportunity for families to unite as a 'family'. God values people and family. The 'noise of this world' is NOT where the presence of God is found.

"And after the earthquake a fire; but the LORD was not in the fire: and after the fire a still small voice" (1 Kings 19:12).

Jeremiah, the 'weeping prophet' wrote, "it is good that a man should both hope, and quietly wait for the salvation of the Lord" (Lamentations 3:26).

Isaiah recognized the power that comes from sitting still in the presence of God:

"Their strength is to sit still" (Isaiah 30:7).

"In returning and rest shall be your strength" (Isaiah 30:15).

Nehemiah, while in exile in Babylon, learned of the dire state of his homeland, Jerusalem. He fasted and prayed and the Lord answered his prayer. He became the instrument of God to assist the people in restoring the walls around the city in his own 'for such a time' moment. When the walls were completed, the people gathered to hear Ezra the priest read the Words of the Lord. God's words caused the people to acknowledge their need for communion with God. The people united and committed to separate themselves and obey God's commandments from their hearts so that they would be able to please God.

What was true then, is also true today. We, too, can experience the fullness and power of God in our life 'for such a time as this". When we are still and listen or read from the Bible, we will learn what is pleasing to God. God will speak to us in 'his still small voice'.

Oftentimes, we as Christians are not even aware that we are spiritually starving from knowing God's word. Would you go a day without eating food? If that is considered by you to be 'unthinkable' (unless you are choosing to 'fast and pray') then why isn't it just as 'unthinkable' to not 'eat' the words from the Bible each day? God blesses those who seek Him. So, make it your 'top priority' every day to read God's words in the

Bible. God will revive our spirit and bring us to confession and worship, and create within us a true passion and love for Him!

It is a choice to daily set aside time to be still and 'read' the Bible. It is those words that give us the strength we need for the challenges we face. Make your first thoughts of the day be about God! **He is faithful and honors those who honor Him.** It is wonderful when we become aware of His Holy Spirit's presence traveling with us. It is prayer that allows us to stay connected with God throughout our day. My friend, Sue, starts her day with praying "**Let** the **words of my mouth**, and the **meditation of my heart**, be acceptable in thy sight, **O LORD**, my strength, and my redeemer" (Psalm 19:14). What a great morning prayer!

Make this prayer and reading the Bible your priority every day as well. Then, go to the Lord and pray about your day, what you need to accomplish, for those that are having problems. Ask the Lord to help them. Simple easy prayers. God promises to hear and answer each prayer in His time and in His way:

'At the **voice of thy cry**, when he shall hear it, he will answer thee" (Isaiah 30:19).

"And thine ears shall hear a word behind thee saying, 'This is the way walk ye in it when ye turn to the right hand and when ye turn to the left" (Isaiah 30:21).

PRAYER: *Lord, forgive me for not desiring to spend more time alone with your Holy Spirit reading your Word the Bible. Please use those very words to touch my heart, and provide me with a fresh new awareness of your presence with your promises to me.*

For Such a Time as This?

Chapter 12

White Linen

Bless the Lord, O my soul, and forget not all His Benefits.

Psalm 103:2

Someday believers will be dressed in white linen in heaven:

"And to her was granted that she should be arrayed in fine linen, clean and white: for the fine linen is the righteousness of saints" (Revelation 19:8).

"White Linen" is actually just a whole lot of 'white crosses' that are weaved together, one small thread at a time, one right after another. The secret to creating a life that is worthy of wearing spiritual 'white linen' is a firm foundation of faith in the Lord. The platform for that firm foundation is found in the book of Isaiah:

For precept must be upon precept, precept upon precept; line upon line, line upon line; here a little, and there a little" (Isaiah 28:10).

We are encouraged by the Lord Jesus Christ to know:

If any man serve me, let him follow me; and where I am, there shall also my servant be: if any man serve me, him will *my* Father honor" (John 12:26).

The steps to placing one line upon another begins with obedience to this truth:

"Therefore, all things whatsoever ye would that men should do to you, do ye even so to them: for this is the law and the prophets" (Mathew 7:12).

The steps to placing precept upon precept begins with yieldedness to this truth:

"Then said Jesus unto his disciples, "If any man will come after me, let him deny himself, and take up his cross, and follow me. For whosoever will save his life shall lose it: and whosoever will lose his life for my sake shall find it. For what is a man profited, if he shall gain the whole world, and lose his own soul? or what shall a man give in exchange for his soul?" (Matthew 16:24-26).

Our attitude must be one of gentleness, love, humility and kindness: rather than caustic humiliation, bitterness, accusation, or judgment.

'Judge not, that ye be not judged. For with what judgment ye judge, ye shall be judged: and with what measure ye mete, it shall be measured to you again. And why beholdest thou the mote that is in thy brother's eye, but considerest not the beam that is in thine own eye? Or how wilt thou say to thy brother, Let me pull out the mote out of thine eye; and, behold, a beam is in thine own eye? Thou hypocrite, first cast out the beam out of thine own eye; and then shalt thou see clearly to cast out the mote out of thy brother's eye" (Matthew 7:1-5).

But the fruit of the Spirit is love, joy, peace, longsuffering, gentleness, goodness, faith, Meekness, temperance: against such there is no law" (Galatians 5:22-23).

Obedience to God's Holy Spirit produces life: Humble yourselves therefore under the mighty hand of God, that he may exalt you in due time: Casting all your care upon him; for He careth for you" (1 Peter 5:6-7). When we take time to read the words written in the Bible, we allow the Lord to 'water' our 'souls' like we would water a seedling. "The cup must be placed under the flow of the water to be filled" Charles Spurgeon, Flowers. The words within the Bible contain the energy of God's Holy Spirit. Just as the sun shines down its rays of sunlight and allows plants to grow, so too, the Lord's Holy Spirit works through the energy of those words, within our hearts, to provide just exactly what we need to thrive and grow strong in the Lord in the power of His might.

We are commanded to GROW: "But grow in grace, and in the knowledge of our Lord and Saviour Jesus Christ. To him be glory both now and for ever. Amen" (1 Peter 3:18).

We are admonished to stay within His precepts of LOVE: God's work is done within our hearts by the Lord: "I am the vine, ye are the branches: He that abideth in me, and I in him, the same bringeth forth much fruit: for without me ye can do nothing" (John 15:5).

We are advised to seek His Will 'first' in our lives: 'But seek ye first the kingdom of God, and his righteousness; and all these things shall be added unto you" (Matthew 6:33).

We are warned to not be deceived: "Wherefore by their fruits ye shall know them. Not every one that saith unto me, Lord, Lord, shall enter into the kingdom of heaven; but he that doeth the will of my Father which is in heaven. Many will say to me in that day, Lord, Lord, have we not prophesied in thy name? And in thy name have cast out devils? and in thy name done many wonderful works? And then will I profess unto them, I never knew you: depart from me, ye that work iniquity. Therefore whosoever heareth these sayings of mine, and doeth them, I will liken him unto a wise man, which built his house upon a rock: And the rain descended, and the floods came, and the winds blew, and beat upon that house; and it fell not: for it was founded upon a rock. And every one that heareth these sayings of mine, and doeth them not, shall be likened unto a foolish man, which built his house upon the sand: And the rain descended, and the floods came, and the winds blew, and beat upon that house; and it fell: and great was the fall of it" (Matthew 7:20-27).

We are instructed to prepare daily to be become vessels for His use:
"Finally, my brethren, be strong in the Lord, and in the power of his might. Put on the whole armour of God, that ye may be able to stand against the wiles of the devil. For we wrestle not against flesh and blood, but against principalities, against powers, against the rulers of the darkness of this world, against spiritual wickedness in high places" (Ephesians 6:10-12).

We are promised someday we will be with Him forever and will proclaim: "Saying, Amen: Blessing, and glory, and wisdom, and thanksgiving, and honour, and power, and might, *be* unto our God for ever and ever. Amen" (Revelation 7:12).

When we faithfully to do our part, He will be faithful to bring us through (not around, or over, or under) the trials that are allowed to come our way that refine our faith, and then provide us with comfort, that we can share with others, who also are asked to go through trials and temptations as well.

It's Just Like Jesus to Drive the Clouds Away – Edna R. Worrell
It's just like Jesus to roll the clouds away,
***It's** just like Jesus to keep me day by day,*
It's just like Jesus all along the way,
It's just like His great love.

PRAYER: Lord help us to be obedient and to trust you in the midst of this trial, to know that you are working this for good, and are behind all things.

Chapter 13

Walls of Protection
"Hid me under the shadow of Thy Wings."

(Psalm 17:8)

Birthdays are special because we take time to think about our lives up until 'now'.

Visualize Your Lifetime

Fabien took a measuring tape one day and asked me to hold one end of it for him. He then walked across the room holding the tape in his hand. He said, "Let me know when you get to your age on the tape and I will stop walking." He walked away from me for quite a distance. When he finally was told to stop, I viewed how far away he was from me. He said, "This represents how old you are." Then he said, "Now, I will walk again, let me know when you reach 85 on the tape." When I told him to stop, he set his end of the measuring tape down, and came and stood beside me. He said, "Look here, this is the amount of time you have left to live if you live to be 85!" I was amazed! This simple exercise had allowed me to 'visualize my lifetime.' I suggest you stop reading, and go and see for yourself what this looks like. It is a true 'eye opener' of the distance we have covered and of what remains to be lived. The comparison of where we have travelled and the remainder of our time here on earth is a BIG wake up moment. Our time remaining on earth is rather short.

Much of life is determined by what we choose to focus upon. It is ironic that it is pride and self-sufficiency that keep us from relying on God for our protection. His 'perfect will' provides us with His Divine protection. The choice is ours to make; to walk alone, or to choose to walk with God. There is a saying, *'What you do speaks so loudly I cannot hear what you are saying."*

When we choose to **neglect reading God's word**, a door is opened for us to travel away from His perfect will.

When we **omit prayer**, the door is open for us to focus on 'serving ourselves' rather than living to 'serve God'.

When **we justify ourselves** in doing so, the door is open for us to literally walk away from the protection of the Lord.

When we **walk away**, the door is open for us to do whatever we please.

There is a downhill slide:

"First neglect, then omission, then treachery, then rebellion" Charles Spurgeon, FLOWERS.

God is ABLE to protect us:

"Fear thou not; for I am with thee: be not dismayed; for I am thy God: I will strengthen thee; yea, I will help thee; yea, I will uphold thee with the right hand of my righteousness" (Isaiah 41:10).

WALLS

Our homes provide us with 'walls of protection' from the wind, water, snow, ice, and cold! So, too, God is able to provide us with a 'spiritual' wall comprised of His angels who are ever working to protect, and keep us from the forces of evil that are in our world. We may not actually get to see an 'angel' but all of us have experienced those 'moments' when we CAN see where we were spared from an accident, or when we were spared from hurting ourselves. When we abide by God's precepts, we will find that we are also spared from the consequences of saying unkind things that hurt not only those we love, but also us. The rule of love is to never start a conversation with a negative, because each conversation we have will never rise above where we begin. If we choose to step 'outside' God's wall of divine protection, we truly step into the unknown. Our words carry power, and sometimes they convey something very different than what we intend to say. Learning and practicing to say 'nothing' rather than say something that we will 'regret' saying is an exercise in discipline. Learning to begin every conversation with words of praise and thanks, is of great benefit to us and those we love. We reaffirm their value to us, and our appreciation for all they do. We are human and we are not perfect. Each of us can choose to be willing to go the 'extra mile' to help rather than condemn, to encourage rather than criticize.

"And whosoever shall compel thee to go a mile, go with him twain" (Matthew 5:42).

"And whatsoever ye do, do it heartily as to the Lord, and not unto men" (Colossians 3:23).

"The LORD is my rock, and my fortress, and my deliverer; my God, my strength, in whom I will trust; my buckler, and the horn of my salvation, and my high tower" (Psalm 18:2).

God's Angels help us:

"The angel of the LORD encampeth round about them that fear him, and delivereth them" (Psalm 34:7).

"No weapon that is formed against thee shall prosper; and every tongue that shall rise against thee in judgment thou shalt condemn. This is the heritage of the servants of the LORD, and their righteousness is of me, saith the LORD"(Isaiah 54:17).

"Every word of God is pure: he is a shield unto them that put their trust in him" (Proverbs 30:5).

"Fear thou not; for I am with thee: be not dismayed; for I am thy God: I will strengthen thee; yea, I will help thee; yea, I will uphold thee with the right hand of my righteousness" (Isaiah 41:10).

A True Account of God's Delightful Provision

My day was going to be full so I got up earlier to make sure I had time to spend reading the Bible before I headed for a trip to town which would include opportunities to drop off fresh garden vegetables to four different friends before going to my dental appointment. On my way into town, I received a call from my cousin Nancy. We had been attempting to get together unsuccessfully. When I was in town, either she was not feeling well, or I was not feeling well enough to visit. But this time, she had received my message that I was headed her way, and she would be available to meet after my dental appointment. My teeth, I was told were in great shape to which I replied, "It is the signature of your dental office that makes that so!" This opened a door for me to share my mini animals and Bible books with several individuals there. Then I headed to visit with Nancy. Nancy's experience provided me with helpful information on how to address a medical issue for which I was truly grateful. She had been going through some of her 'possessions' and had several bags set aside for me and my family. We went through the bags of clothing and other things in the bags, and I loaded them into me car as we parted and agreed to meet again soon. On my way home I prayed about who to 'gift' these earthly goods to: there were frames, perfume, socks, clothing, a leaf pillow and runner that matched, and many other lovely things! My first stop was to one of my sister's April, who agreed that the frames could be used, as she did picture framing for others. My next stop was to visit my sister Dayle, who I knew loved perfumes and socks. When I handed her the bag of perfumes, she went through the bottles, exclaiming, "These cost $100 a bottle! Are you sure Nancy's wants to give them away?" I assured her Nancy did, and asked if she would like some wonderful socks as well. She replied, "I just gave away a ton of indoor plants for free, and this is definitely coming back to me today in a different form, of something that I really love – perfume and socks! Thank you, Jesus!" When I brought in the bag of socks, there were also a couple of pairs of pants in the bag, and those fit her perfectly. We both were excited to have connected again with Nancy and for her generosity! Then I was off to see another sister, Trey. When I arrived, I gave her mail to her from the Post Office, and said, "I have some things from Nancy for you. I thought of you right away when she gave me a leaf pillow and leaf table runner, I know you love fall leaves." As I pulled both out of the bag, my sister said, "Did you know about what we did today?" I replied, "No, what did you do today?" She answered, "We waxed leaves, and framed them, come and see!" I followed as she took me to a wall where a frame was hung with beautiful fall colored leaves that matched the pillow and the runner perfectly! The synergy of "God's Amazing Ways" was not lost on me, nor on my family members. When we are about His business, we will be full of Praise for we will witness first hand God's goodness and grace. The Lord is delighted when we choose to bless one another.

God is able to provide for all our needs (as well as some of our wants):
We are told to, "Cast all your care upon Him, for He careth for you" (1 Peter 5:7).

".. with purpose of heart . . . cleave to the Lord" (Acts 11:23).

"He giveth power to the faint, and to them that have no might" (Isaiah 40:29).

"The Lord knoweth the way" (Psalm 11:6).

"Hide me under the shadow of Thy wings: (Psalm 17:8).

Jesus *IS* Coming

Not many Christians realize how very close we are to the return of Jesus in the air for His own. The Lord continues to show me which makes me desire to use every minute that I can to witness, pray and read and study the Bible. The most wonderful thing of all is God is able to change us from the inside out:

"A new heart also will I give you, and a new spirit will I put within you: and I will take away the stony heart out of your flesh, and I will give you a heart of flesh" (Ezekiel 36:26).

"These things are written that ye may KNOW that ye have eternal life" (1 John 5:13).

"What shall we then say to these things? If God be for us, who can be against us?" (Romans 8:31).

"Now unto him that is able to do exceeding abundantly above all that we ask or think, according to the power that worketh in us, unto him be glory in the church by Christ Jesus throughout all ages, world without end. Amen" (Ephesians 3:20-21).

"Some trust in chariots, and some in horses: but we will remember the name of the LORD our God" (Psalm 20:7).

PRAYER:

Lord help us to recognize that happiness comes from having your presence within our life!

Thank you for the unexpected blessings that you bring upon us that encourage us and strengthen our faith!

For Such a Time as This?

Chapter 14

Please God

Let the words of my mouth and the medication of my heart be pleasing in thy sight, O Lord, my strength and my redeemer.

Psalm 19:14

When we value God, our true value will be made known to us. God loves and treasures us so much that He purchased us back.

None of us is 'good enough' to enter the perfection of heaven. Living in heaven requires forgiveness, and receiving eternal life. Jesus referred to this as being 'born again'. This brings a joy that passes all understanding, and opens a door for unexpected delights from the Lord.

My life was totally changed when I literally 'turned around' after I had walked away from God. I was determined to never go back to a church. I was 'done' the message of Jesus being the 'only way' could NOT possibly be correct! As I walked away, the Lord spoke right to me. His voice was very clear, "If you walk away now, you will be on your own." That is all that was said. I remember standing still for just a moment, and literally pivoting my feet and walking back into the church. I walked up to Joyce Carruth the pastor's wife and stated, "I need to ask Jesus to come into my life to help me, but I don't know what to say." Joyce helped me to pray. I did repeat a prayer. I said, "I believe Jesus you came; I believe you died, and I believe you rose again. Please forgive me and come into my life." Tears gushed out and I sobbed in relief as I felt God's Holy Spirit come into my body. The Lord whispered, "Your life will not be easy, but you'll never walk alone!" That was on April 13, 1975, over 45 years ago. My life has been challenging, and unpredictable, but the Lord has been very faithful to me. I have walked away from him, and returned many times. He has been faithful to never leave me, to always come to look for me, and to be there for me to help me get out of the messes I have gotten into from exercising my own self will, apart from stopping and praying and asking Him to help me.

"Likewise, joy shall be in heaven over one sinner that repenteth"

(Luke 15: 7).

HEAVEN CAME DOWN AND GLORY FILLED MY SOUL

O what a wonderful, wonderful day - day I will never forget;
After I'd wandered in darkness away, Jesus my Saviour I met.
O what a tender, compassionate friend - He met the need of my heart;
Shadows dispelling, With joy I am telling, He made all the darkness depart.

Heaven came down and glory filled my soul,
When at the cross the Saviour made me whole;
My sins were washed away -
And my night was turned to day -
Heaven came down and glory filled my soul!

Born of the Spirit with life from above into God's fam'ly divine,
Justified fully thru Calvary's love, O what a standing is mine!
And the transaction so quickly was made when as a sinner I came,
Took of the offer of grace He did proffer - He saved me, O praise His dear name! John W. Peterson (1921- 2006)

PRAYER: Lord help me to be sensitive to your Holy Spirit and to be willing to NOT lean unto my own understanding, Rather help me to stop and pray and seek you will.

Chapter 15

Have Faith

And whatsoever ye shall ask in my name, that will I do, that the Father may be glorified in the Son. If ye shall ask any thing in my name, I will do *It*. If ye love me, keep my commandments.
John 14: 13-15

God's promises are real. God is able to do abundantly above all we can ask or think (Ephesians 3:20). There are some prayers that are answered immediately, others take a few days, some weeks, some months, some years. The most amazing part of prayer is that the Lord answers prayer and He is so FAITHFUL!

A Lovely Surprise

Valentine's Day is one day that I like to be able to do something special for Fabien. My prayer was to the Lord for something that would be unusual, yet meaningful, and that would cost little to nothing. My goal was to convey my appreciation to him and for his presence in my life.

Knowing meals mean a lot to him, I decided to make him deviled eggs. I boiled up a dozen of them. As I cut them in half to remove the center yolks, I was amazed with what one of those eggs had inside. As I opened it up, I looked and there in front of me was a perfectly formed 'heart' shaped yolk, on both sides. One of the sides actually had the white of the egg that was formed into a 'heart' shape as well. I had to stand there and look at this sight again and again, to convince myself that what I was actually seeing was 'real'. This egg yolk would not be removed. It would remain as it was so that when I gave Fabien his plate of food, I could place the special 'heart' egg on his plate. I told him, "And here is something extra special for your for-Valentine's Day!" As he looked at the heart shaped yoke inside the egg, he exclaimed, "Well, that must have been a really happy chicken to lay such a 'Lovely Egg"!"

"Yes, indeed!", I replied! We both laughed and I took time to take a picture of the heart shaped egg so I could share the wonder of the Lord's ability to answer a unique prayer in a very special way!

Importunity

The experience with the 'heart shaped egg' is what happens when we pray. The Lord will give us the desires of our heart. But regardless of whether the Lord answers right away or delays an answer we are to be 'importunate" in prayer.

'Importunate' is to be undiscouraged by delayed answers to prayers. Be willing to ask again and again. The Lord promises that "the fervent persistent prayer' of a righteous man is heard in heaven. "Yet because of his importunity' he will rise and give him" (Luke 11:8).

Right Hand/Left Hand

When you are praying and walking in obedience to God's leading, we are instructed to be aware that we are still living in bodies made of flesh, and like 'oil' and 'water' – things of the Spirit and things of the flesh do not mix. Those who value this world and the things of this world more than then they value a relationship with God, are often unable to appreciate the things of God.

"But when thou doest alms, **let not thy left hand know** what **thy right hand** doeth: that thine alms **may** be in secret: and **thy** Father which seeth in secret himself **shall** reward thee openly" (Matthew 6:3-4).

The left hand is the 'flesh'; the right hand is "spirit".

Therefore, be not distressed when people criticize you or even yell at you; be more concerned with pleasing God.

When we do nothing difficult, controversial or upsetting we need not be worried. Those who are more 'concerned' about the things of this world alone, will not judge us. But exercise your Faith in God, and man's judgements will follow:

"If the world hate you, ye know that it hated me before it hated you. If ye were of the world, the world would love his own: but because ye are not of the world, but I have chosen you out of the world, therefore the world hateth you. Remember the word that I said unto you, the servant is not greater than his lord. If they have persecuted me, they will also persecute you; if they have kept my saying, they will keep yours also" (John 15:15-20).

We are Encouraged to Have Courage

Remember, courage is when we do something in spite of our fears. It is taking action in obedience to His leading and not being dismayed even if we are judged by men who are not in 'tune' and who do not have spiritual eyes to see our understand.

"Be of good courage, and He shall strengthen your heart, all ye that hope in the Lord: (Psalm 31:24).

"If I yet pleased **men**, I should not be the servant of Christ"

(Galatians 1:10).

"Now unto him that is able to do exceedingly abundantly above all that we ask or think according to the power that worketh in us, unto him be glory in the church by Christ Jesus throughout all ages, world without end.

Amen" (Ephesians 3:20-21).

Delight thyself also in the LORD: and he shall give thee the desires of **thine** heart" (Psalm 37:4).

Take my Life and Let it Be

> Take my life and let it be
> Consecrated, Lord, to Thee.
> Take my moments and my days,
> Let them flow in endless praise.
> Take my hands and let them move
> At the impulse of Thy love.
> Take my feet and let them be
> Swift and beautiful for Thee.
> Take my voice and let me sing,
> Always, only for my King.
> Take my lips and let them be
> Filled with messages from Thee.
> Take my silver and my gold,
> Not a mite would I withhold.
> Take my intellect and use
> Every pow'r as Thou shalt choose.
> Take my will and make it Thine,
> It shall be no longer mine.
> Take my heart, it is Thine own,
> It shall be Thy royal throne.
> Take my love, my Lord, I pour
> At Thy feet its treasure store.
> Take myself and I will be
> Ever, only, all for Thee.   Francis Havergal 1874

PRAYER: *Lord help us to not shortchange ourselves from experiencing the 'smiles' that come from heaven. Help us to be willing to walk in obedience to the leading of your Holy Spirit. Help us to want to be available to be your vessel: to be your hands, feet, ears, eyes, and mouth. Lord meet us there in your amazingly wonderful ways.*

Chapter 16

Wait

"For he is not a God of the dead, but of the living: for all live unto him."

Luke 20:38

When we determine to assess our lives based upon only what we can 'understand' during our moments of crisis or trial, we rob ourselves of having 'peace' in the midst of the storm.

The greatest gift the Lord gives us is His ability to give His peace when we bring our concerns to the Lord in prayer. This is a peace that surpasses our ability to understand. The Bible is full of accounts of how God did in deed 'work things together for good' (Romans 8:28).

Victory Through Grace

Not to the strong is the battle, not to the swift is the race,

Yet to the true and the faithful vict'ry is promised through grace.

Frances J. Crosby 1890

"Wherefore seeing we also are compassed about with so great a cloud of witnesses, let us lay aside every weight, and the sin which doth so easily beset us, and let us run with patience the race that is set before us,

Looking unto Jesus the author and finisher of our faith; who for the joy that was set before him endured the cross, despising the shame, and is set down at the right hand of the throne of God.

For consider him that endured such contradiction of sinners against himself, lest ye be wearied and faint in your minds" (Hebrews 12:1-3).

Blessed shall we be if we are enabled to imitate the example of the Lord Jesus who served the Father in the spirit of Sonship. Love made him

rise above all idea of present recompense: He waited the Father's time, and he still waits for his complete reward until the hour of his Second Advent shall arrive."

Charles Spurgeon "Flowers" P. 222

We, are human, we are not God. We cannot understand 'eternity' within the present 'time' in which we live. We can only receive what He is doing by faith in what He has promised is to come.

Wait on the Lord, be of good courage, and He shall strengthen thine heart: Wait I say on the Lord" (Psalm 27:14).

PRAYER:

Lord help me to care more about my relationship with you than anything else, for I will live with you forever in eternity! Help me to indeed seek first the Kingdom of God and His Righteousness.

Have mercy on me for my own lack of faith in your ability to work all for 'good' and help me to WAIT for you to create change within our hearts in your time and in your way!

Chapter 17

Don't Quit

For nothing is secret, that shall not be made manifest; neither anything hid, that shall not be known and come abroad.
(Jesus)

Luke 8:17

The best advice I ever received was, "Just keep your head down, and keep moving forward!" Instructions for the battlefield of life! My husband Fabien calls it, "Hitting bottom." The end of pride and self-sufficiency where we admit we need help.

Don't Quit
by
John Greenleaf Whittier
When things go wrong as they sometimes will,
When the road you're trudging seems all up hill,
When the funds are low and the debts are high
And you want to smile, but you have to sigh,
When care is pressing you down a bit,
Rest if you must, but don't you quit.
Life is strange with its twists and turns
As every one of us sometimes learns
And many a failure comes about
When he might have won had he stuck it out;
Don't give up though the pace seems slow—
You may succeed with another blow.
Success is failure turned inside out—
The silver tint of the clouds of doubt,
And you never can tell just how close you are,
It may be near when it seems so far;
So stick to the fight when you're hardest hit—
It's when things seem worst that you must not quit.

Working through to the End

One of my own 'Don't Quit' accounts occurred after I had fallen and broken my right arm. After six months of Physical Therapy (PT) my arm was no better than when we started. Surgery was scheduled which would require another six months of PT therapy after the surgery for full mobility to be restored. I cried when I was told the news, but my close friend encouraged me to not loose hope. The surgery went well, and the PT therapy began, being done morning and night. This involved my lying on the floor every day and having my friend push up on my arm to get it to move to the top position close to my neck, and in front of me over my head. The arm would not budge past the half-way point. After more than six months of working on it, I determined that the daily exercises were a waste of our time, and that I would have to learn to live with what mobility I did have. I determined to not do exercises any more. But my friend insisted I continue the exercises, and would not let me 'quit'. It was a total shock to me when within a few days after making my ultimatum, as my friend pushed, it suddenly released through the interior barrier and I had full mobility of my arm up close to my neck and above my head. We sat together just amazed. I was truly speechless as I realized how close I was to success; when I felt I was never going to make it! Since then, this experience has helped me many times to 'continue' as I KNOW what I THINK I know -- I just don't really know. So, never 'Quit'. Keep at it, and you, too, will be shocked and awed at the results of exercising persistence in the presence of what seems immovable.

The work of this life is to 'align' and become 'obedient to' the Lord Jesus

Christ and the leading of His Holy Spirit. We have total forgiveness and assurance of being an 'heir' of 'eternal life' through faith in Jesus Christ.

Jesus

During the three years that Jesus ministered on earth, his message was to have faith in God, to put God first, and to love others. When Jesus was on the cross, one of the two thieves turned and said, "Remember me, when I come into your Kingdom!" Jesus replied, "Today, thou shalt be with me in paradise!" From the cross, Jesus also proclaimed, "It is Finished!" and "Forgive them, for they know not what they do" and "Into Thy hands I commend my Spirit". Jesus' Spirit left his body, he died. The guard used a sword and pushed it through his side, and water and blood came out. Jesus exited his physical body at His command, the sky turned as black as night, and there was a great earthquake, and the Temple curtain was split in two within the inner sanctuary - direct access to God had been provided for all! The guard proclaimed, "Surely, this was the Son of God!" Graves opened and spirits appeared to many within the city. Pilate allowed Joseph and Nicodemus to take Jesus down and place him in Joseph's tomb. On the third day, while the tomb was heavily guarded, there was another great earthquake. The stone rolled way. When the three women left early on the third day to anoint his body, they wondered how they would roll the stone away, and were shocked when they found the tomb open. Two returned to tell the others, but Mary remained behind crying, she saw a man she thought was the gardener, and asked, 'Where have ye taken him?" He replied, "Mary'. Immediately she knew it was Jesus When she tried to embrace Jesus, he replied,

'Touch me not, for I have not yet ascended to my Father and your Father, but go and tell the brethren and Peter, that I have risen." Mary's message was met by disbelieve by the disciples. But John and Peter were compelled to go and see. They found the tomb as Mary said. Empty. This account is contained in all of the four gospels: Matthew, Mark, Luck and John. Jesus appeared and disappeared many times within 40 days following His resurrection. Finally, Jesus appeared before 500 people gathered on the Mount of Olives. A cloud circled his feet, and he gave the great commission to go and tell everyone the good news. Then he was taken up into heaven. When the people stayed and stared looking up, two men came down in white apparel and told them to go and do as Jesus commanded. This account is contained in the book of Acts.

He has promised: "I will never leave you, nor forsake you" (Hebrews 13:5)

PRAYER:

Truly Lord, I do not feel equipped for this journey, but I place my hand in yours and I ask that you cover me with your precious blood and guide my thoughts and actions. Help me to trust you and do the work that is before me, even when it seems like there is no end to it all. Remind me that there is indeed an 'end' and that your promises are true.

Chapter 18

Abide

Abide in me, and I in you.
As the branch cannot bear fruit of itself, except it abide on the vine;
no more can ye, except ye abide in me.

John 15:4

Opportunities abound for each of us to touch the lives of others with words of kindness, love and encouragement. Romans 12 compares 'abiding' with God and others as it is for us to be in our physical body. Our body has many parts but all of those parts work together to allow us to physically function. When you stop and think about it, it is absolutely jaw dropping amazing! Each breath requires our lungs to take in air and release air, to enable our heart to beat that pumps our blood through our veins, throughout our bodies depositing nutrients and removing toxicity. The food we eat is processed within our stomach, then it takes a ride to provide the nutrients we require for good health, our system removes what we don't need through our liver and kidneys for exiting our system. Everything is connected to everything else: my eyes, ears, nose, mouth, my hands my feet, all must work together for me to able to function and move around. Our environment shouts to us of the miraculous Creator who uses sun, water, and air to give life, food, and pleasure.

It only takes a small 'cut' for us to realize how quickly our entire body responds to pain. When we hurt either physically or emotionally, we impact those around us.

"For in Him we live and move and have our being" (Acts 17:28).

"I beseech you therefore, brethren, by the mercies of God, that ye present your bodies a living sacrifice, holy, acceptable unto God, which is your reasonable service.
And be not conformed to this world: but be ye transformed by the renewing of your mind, that ye may prove what is that good, and acceptable, and perfect, will of God" (Romans 12: 1-2).

And we are members of one another with different gifts:
Prophecy- according to the proportion of our Faith
Ministry - let us wait on our ministry
Teaching – let us wait on our teaching
Exhortation – Let us wait
Give with simplicity
Rule– with diligence
Have Mercy with cheerfulness
Love without dissimulation
Abhor evil; cleave to good
Be Kind to one another preferring one another
Be not slothful but fervent in spirit serving God
Rejoice in Hope
Be Patient in Tribulation
Be Instant in Prayer
Distribute to the necessities of saints
Given to hospitality
Bless and curse not

Rejoice with them that rejoice

Weep with them that weep

Be of the same mind toward another

Mind not high things but condescend to men of low estate

Be not wise in your own conceits

Recompense to no man evil

Provide things honest in the sight of all men

Live peaceably with all men

Give not place unto wrath

Overcome evil with good

We are further instructed to, "add to your faith virtue, and to virtue knowledge, and to knowledge temperance, and to temperance patience and to patience godliness, and to godliness brotherly kindness and to brotherly kindness, charity" (2 Peter 1:5-7).

"The steps of a good man are ordered by the Lord and he delighted in His way" (Psalm 37:23).

PRAYER:
Lord help us to 'trust' that you are indeed in control, and to wait for your perfect timing. Give us the ability to exercise the gifts you have given us and to recognize that everyone is different, that we are to become a Spiritual body united in faith, hope and love.

For Such a Time as This?

Chapter 19

Look Ahead

For the Son of man shall come in the glory of his Father with his angels; and then he shall reward every man according to his works.

Matthew 16:27

There was a time in my life when I actually owned and rode a motorcycle. In order to obtain a license to ride, I had to complete a written test as well as participate in a weekend riding course. During that course, I learned one very important lesson.

When riding a motorcycle, it is CRITICAL to LOOK where you WANT to go, not where you are at! To successfully ride around corners in the road, your eyes must look through the corner, ahead to where you want to go. A motorcycle will go where you are looking.

The danger is if you stop and look at where you are at any time during the 'turn' within a corner in a road, the motorcycle starts to go exactly where you are looking, and that can bring you right into the ditch.

This reality is true for our spiritual walk with the Lord as well. This is what it means to walk by FAITH and not by SIGHT. It is our 'spiritual view' that allows us to remain on the 'highway of our God' headed in the right direction. When we see life events from an eternal view, we gain the ability to see differently. Each trial will eventually reveal to us a spiritual truth that we would not 'see' any other way. Even illnesses provide us with a new level of compassion for those who suffer. They also reveal that 'health' itself is an incredible gift from God to us for which we need to be thankful and grateful.

The Beatitudes

Jesus gave very important instructions for 'looking ahead' within the Beatitudes from His sermon on the mount to 5,000 people.

The first four Beatitudes 'Look towards God':

Blessed are the poor in spirit: for theirs is the kingdom of heaven.
This requires our Humility.

Blessed are they that mourn: for they shall be comforted.
This requires our Repentance.

Blessed are the meek: for they shall inherit the earth.
This produces our Salvation.

Blessed are they which do hunger and thirst after righteousness: for they shall be filled.
This produces our Sanctification.

The next 4 Beatitudes 'Look towards others':

Blessed are the merciful: for they shall obtain mercy.
This requires God's mercy working through us.

Blessed are the pure in heart: for they shall see God.
This requires us to focus on God.

Blessed are the peacemakers: for they shall be called the children of God.
This requires us to become peacemakers.

Blessed are they which are persecuted for righteousness' sake: for theirs is the kingdom of heaven.
This requires us to become forgivers.

His last Instruction Looks towards Eternity and the Future:
Blessed are ye, when men shall revile you, and persecute you, and shall say all manner of evil against you falsely, for my sake. Rejoice, and be exceeding glad: for great is your reward in heaven: for so persecuted they the prophets which were before you. Ye are the salt of the earth: but if the salt have lost his savour, wherewith shall it be salted? it is thenceforth good for nothing, but to be cast out, and to be trodden under foot of men. Ye are the light of the world. A city that is set on an hill cannot be hid. Neither do men light a candle, and put it under a bushel, but on a candlestick; and it giveth light unto all that are in the house. Let your light so shine before men, that they may see your good works, and glorify your Father which is in heaven. Think not that I am come to destroy the law, or the prophets: I am not come to destroy, but to fulfil. For verily I say unto you, Till heaven and earth pass, one jot or one tittle shall in no wise pass from the law, till all be fulfilled.

Matthew 5: 2-18

His goal is for us to be 'vessels' for His use to share His light and love. We begin with our 'new birth' just like a new green leaf, fresh out of its seed pod. As we pray, and turn to the Lord, we are changed, and transformed into the image of God's love

The "Light" contained in His words in the Bible are what is used to show us where the next step is, and then the next, and the next. The journey is "One Day at a Time", not looking behind, but 'looking ahead' to the next step. Just as the Israelites were guided though the wilderness:

"The Lord alone did lead them" (Deuteronomy 32:12).

Psalm 37 has specific instructions for looking ahead:

Trust

Delight

Commit

Rest

Wait patiently for Him

Fret not thyself

Wait on the Lord

The Lord WILL help and deliver.

The steps of a good man are ordered by the LORD: and he delighteth in his way. Though he fall, he shall not be utterly cast down: for the LORD upholdeth him with his hand" (Psalm 37: 23-24).

"For we are His workmanship, created in Christ Jesus unto good works, which God hath before ordained that we should walk in them" (Ephesians 2:10).

Divine transformation is a process which takes time.

There is coming a day when we will be asked to give an account to the Lord of what we have done during our days on earth. Therefore:

"Whatsoever ye do, do it heartily unto the Lord and not unto men; knowing that of the Lord ye shall receive the reward of the inheritance: for ye serve the Lord Christ" (Colossians 3:23-24)

Jesus had his last words on the cross, "Father forgive them for they know not what they do" (Luke 23:24). So:

"Love your enemies, bless them that curse you, do good to them that hate you, and pray for them which despitefully use you, and persecute you; that he may be the children of your Father which is in heaven: for He maketh His sun to rise on the evil and on the good, and sendeth rain on the just and on the unjust" (Matthew 5:45).

Believes are promised that we will be redeemed and taken off the earth before the time of 'Jacob's trouble" begins. Then after the 'rapture' of believers from all denominations, there will be allowed seven years for people on earth to legislate 'peace' which will result in war. Then, before the earth is destroyed, the Lord Jesus Christ will return to earth and will rule and reign on earth for 1,000 years. We are told to comfort one another with these words:

"For the Lord himself shall descend from heaven with a shout, with the voice of the archangel, and with the trump of God; and the dead in Christ shall rise first, then we which are alive and remain shall be caught up together with them in the clouds, to meet the Lord in the air, and so shall we ever be with the Lord. Wherefore comfort one another with these words" (1 Thessalonians 4:16-18).

So, look ahead, so you may make the most of each day. So, look ahead and do not put off doing things until tomorrow. Often, things can seem much larger in our 'mind' than they really are in reality. Because **one day**, we will find ourselves, rather unexpectedly in His Presence - forever!

PRAYER:

Lord, give us VISION, help us to trust you to direct our path, and to keep taking the next step, and the next, and the next. And help us to not worry about what people think about us, but rather help us to be obedient to you.

Chapter 20

Remembrance

His ways are everlasting.

Habakkuk 3:6

"Then they that **feared** the LORD spake often one to another: and the LORD hearkened, and heard it, and a book of remembrance was written before him for them that feared the LORD, and that thought upon his name.

And they shall be mine, saith the LORD of hosts, in that day when I make up my jewels; and I will spare them, as a man spareth his own son that serveth him. Then shall ye return, and discern between the righteous and the wicked, between him that serveth God and him that serveth him not" (Malachi 16:18).

Life is NOT meant to be easy. Jesus was very clear, "These things I have spoken unto you, that in me ye might have peace. In the world ye shall have tribulation: but be of good cheer; I have overcome the world" (Matthew 16:33). Challenges can arrive as small, medium, large, extra-large, as well as beyond our imagination complicated! The Lord takes all of these as moments that allow us to connect with Him. One time I was asked to participate in a conference call for my work. The call involved five participants including myself. The outcome of the call, was unknown but would have a large impact on my future. I begin my days with prayer for the day. As this particular day wore on, my anxiety level rose every time I thought and wondered about the call's outcome. Each time, I stopped and prayed and asked the Lord to help me let go and to trust Him. I asked Him to help me to remember that He is indeed in control of all things. I reminded myself that no matter how things turned out, it would be according to His will. I repeated the prayer Jesus said before he was betrayed by Judas in the garden, 'not my will but thine be done."

The call was scheduled for 3 pm Jesus prayed three times the same words before his arrest; I now prayed that same prayer three times. Again, I asked the Lord to help me to remember that He was in control of all things. I asked God to help me to know what to say and what not to say during the conference call and for peace within my heart and mind. My level of peace came and went all day, and my prayers continued throughout the day to counterbalance my anxieties.

About five minutes before the call, my neighbor Virginia arrived home and met my husband Fabien outside in our front yard. She handed him a gift that was for me. Fabien rushed into the house and handed me that gift of a hippopotamus figurine. He exclaimed, "This is from Virginia for you!" Then told me the story of where it came from. "When Virginia was in a store today someone in front of her in line was going to purchase this, but when the clerk dropped it onto the floor, its lower foot was chipped off. Then that woman said, "I don't want it, it's broken." Virginia was right behind her in line. When she saw that the clerk was going to throw it away. Virginia exclaimed, "I'll take it!" Then, the clerk just handed the hippopotamus to her and said, "No charge!"

The hippopotamus had a cap on with the word "Play". What I saw was "PRAY". The hippo was sitting, and had five playing cards in its hands.

Tears came into my eyes. As I placed the hippo beside my laptop, I understood that the 5 participants in my call were all in the hands of God, and that the outcome was already known to God. Jesus's outcome had also been determined according to God's will. Great peace flooded my soul. I entered the call, calm and composed. Finally, at the end of the call, I was asked to talk about the issues. Amazingly, the solutions I proposed were totally accepted. One of my closing remarks had everyone who had been very tense, laughing together.

After the call, I immediately went and thanked Virginia for the gift. She then told me how odd it was that she received that hippo. How she got to say, "I'll take it!" and received it at no cost. Virginia knew my affinity to hippopotamuses and has gifted me one almost every year, but typically she has had to search to find them. I got to explain how the Lord planned the arrival of that hippopotamus just before my conference call, which was an answered prayer providing peace to participate in that call.

Since that time, that hippopotamus resides as a visual remembrance on my work desk of the power of the Lord to hear and answer prayer.

We are promised:

There hath no temptation taken you but such as is common to man: but God is faithful, who will not suffer you to be tempted above that ye are able; but will with the temptation also make a way to escape, that ye may be able to bear it" (1 Corinthians 10:13).

We are assured:

"I am Alpha and Omega, the beginning and the ending, saith the Lord, which is, and which was, and which is to come, the Almighty" (Rev. 1:8).

For Such a Time as This?

"Trust in the LORD with all thine heart; and lean not unto thine own understanding. [6] In all thy ways acknowledge him, and he shall direct thy paths" (Proverbs 3:4-5)

We have assurance that the Lord hears our every prayer no matter the challenge. Our task is to PRAY and leave the outcomes of circumstances beyond our control, with Him.

Prayer transports us into the 'eye' of a storm. God's peace is possible even in the midst of 'unknowns' in non-understandable ways.

God can arrange an odd chain of events, with perfect timing, for a specific outcome. He brought Virginia to that particular store, placed her in line right behind the woman, who serendipitously found that hippopotamus, had a clerk accidently drop it, and had Virginia in the right place at the right time, to be present to receive it and then hand it to my husband, who brought it to me just 5 minutes before that important life impacting phone call. How amazingly wonderful is that!?? People right where they needed to be doing things for which they had no idea of the cascading end result of just 'one answered prayer'. This produces such an awareness of His majesty that my heart MUST give Him praise and glory for: WHO He is!!, and for WHAT he is able to do!

Help us Lord to be strong in the grace, that is in Christ Jesus, to live DEAD to this world and ALIVE to God. Let Christ be ALL, and in ALL.

Help us Lord to put on "bowels of mercies, kindness, humbleness of mind, meekness, longsuffering, forbearing one another, and forgiving one another, and help us to forgive 'even as Christ forgave'; help us to 'put on charity, which is the bond of perfectness' and let 'the peace of God rule in our heart'. Help us to be' one body' and to be 'THANKFUL'.

"May the word of Christ dwell in us richly in all wisdom, teaching and admonishing one another in psalms and hymns and spiritual songs, singing with grace in our heart as to the Lord; and whatsoever we do in word or deed, let us do all in the name of the Lord Jesus giving thanks to God the Father by Him; whatsoever we do, help us to do it heartily as to the Lord, and not unto men, knowing that of the Lord we shall receive the reward of the inheritance for we serve the Lord Christ" (Colossians 3:16).

PRAYER:

*Help us to **remember** that no one is out of God's sight and help us to give you all PRAISE, GLORY and HONOR – for ever and ever.*

Chapter 21

Silver and Gold
I go to prepare a place for you.

(John 14:1)

The place Jesus has gone to prepare for us is free from sorrow, tears, and suffering. It is a place where all things are made new.

"I am the Alpha and the Omega, the beginning and the End, the first and the last" (Revelation 22:12).

That is what we are being prepared 'for' by the Lord. Our part is to ask the Lord for His guidance, His wisdom, and His understanding.

The words we will say to the Lord when we meet Him face-to-face have meaning. We will declare that He is:

BLESSING and GLORY – Because both are His, and they are His to give!

WISDOM and UNDERSTANDING – Because he knows everything!

And HONOR – Because honor belongs to Him for Who He is: Our Creator!

And POWER – Because all Power Belongs to Him!

And MIGHT – Because He gives us 'His Holy Spirit's' presence moment by moment which enables us to be equipped for His purpose!

"By wisdom a **house** is **built**, and by understanding it is established; by **knowledge** the rooms are filled with all precious and pleasant riches" (Proverbs 24: 3-4).

Earthly wisdom allows designs on earth to be made.

Heavenly wisdom allows us to see what needs to be done.

Earthly understanding allows things to be established.

Godly understanding allows us to apply God's principles to our life.

Earthly knowledge produces productivity and tangible products.

Godly knowledge takes understanding and wisdom and produces tangible love, joy, peace, longsuffering, gentleness, goodness and faith.

The Dream

One night, I had a dream about 'silver' and 'gold'.

Silver was presented as FORGIVENESS

Gold was presented as LOVE

The gifts of both LOVE and FORGIVENESS come from the Lord who seeks to bestow these upon us, but we are given the choice to accept or reject these gifts from Him. When we choose to receive them, we are empowered to use them to help others. Receiving requires humility. Receiving and giving to others also requires humility.

In the dream I understood that it took faith and courage to receive the gifts. In my dream, I was in a church and everyone was there looking for LOVE and FORGIVENESS but no one seemed to understand how to obtain either. The message was that in order to receive them, we needed to have an attitude of 'not being concerned what people thought'. Our focus and concern needed to be centered upon God, to ask Him to forgive us and come into our heart. All of us saw that pride and fear prevented us from receiving God's gift of forgiveness. Even in churches, the enemy can distract us and dazzle us with 'wonderful works' that catch our 'eyes' and divert our attention away from God. God desires that our focus be upon the Lord Jesus Christ. Our faith in Him and acknowledgement of our need for His forgiveness provides us access to God's Holy Spirit.

PRAYER:

Lord, thank you and praise you, that you have provided the tools we need to be successful in your work of giving your love to one another. Help us Lord to come to you with our concerns, to pray for your help to us to love ourselves, and to accept your forgiveness, which you give freely to us, when we humbly come before your presence, and ask for it.

For Such a Time as This?

Chapter 22

The Overcomer

Be of good cheer; I have overcome the world.

(Jesus)

John 16:33

While we are on this earth, we have an opportunity to glorify the Lord in eternity by allowing His Holy Spirit to dwell within us. Every day we may become His hands and His feet. We can be available to the Lord for His Heavenly business!

The outcomes of 9/11, the pestilence of COVID19, along with other natural disasters, provide a platform where we can focus our time and talents to share the love of God and the message of Jesus Christ. God is in control of **all things** and will indeed work "all things together for good" (Romans 8:28).

The Biblical eternal perspective provides redemption for us through Jesus Christ, by God Himself, through the indwelling of His Holy Spirit. Jesus Christ's ministry on earth lasted 3 years. When we add the 40 days between Jesus' resurrection and His ascension (Acts 1:3) to the total length of Jesus' earthly ministry, from His baptism to His ascension, beginning in AD 26 to the spring of AD30; we have approximately 3½ years.

Jesus's ultimate prayer to God was one of yieldedness to His divine earthly purpose: "Not my will, but thine be done" (Luke 22:42).

After he uttered those words, "there appeared an angel unto him from heaven strengthening Him" (Luke 22:43).

Before Jesus went to the cross, he declared that He would be resurrected from the dead. "Destroy this temple, and in **three days I will** raise it **up**" (**John** 2:19). Jesus was indeed raised from the dead. There was no body found within the tomb, only the burial clothes.

"Now the next day, that followed the **day of** the preparation, the chief priests and Pharisees came together unto Pilate, Saying, Sir, we remember that that deceiver said, while he was yet alive, **After three days I will rise again.** Pilate said unto them, Ye have a watch: go your way, make it as sure as ye can" (Mathew 27:63).

"Now upon the first day of the week, very early in the morning, they came unto the sepulchre, bringing the spices which they had prepared, and certain others with them. And they found the stone rolled away from the sepulchre. And they entered in, and found not the body of the Lord Jesus. And it came to pass, as they were much perplexed thereabout, behold, two men stood by them in shining garments: And as they were afraid, and bowed down their faces to the earth, they said unto them, **why seek ye the living among the dead?** He is not here, but is risen: remember how he spake unto you when he was yet in Galilee, Saying, The Son of man must be delivered into the hands of sinful men, and be crucified, and the third day rise again. And they remembered his words, and returned from the sepulchre, and told all these things unto the eleven, and to all the rest" (Luke 24: 1-9).

Jesus's After Death Appearances

Jesus is recorded as appearing physically alive to his disciples and others after his resurrection in his resurrected body:

To Mary Magdalene:

Jesus said to her, "Mary." She turned and said to him in Hebrew, "Rabboni!" (which means Teacher). Jesus said to her, "Do not hold me, for I have not yet ascended to the Father; but go to my brethren and say to them, I am ascending to my Father and your Father, to my God and your God." (John 20:16-17)

To Other Women (possibly Mary of Clopas, Mary the mother of James and Joanna):

So, they departed quickly from the tomb with fear and great joy, and ran to tell his disciples. And behold, Jesus met them and said, "Hail!" And they came up and took hold of his feet and worshiped him. Then Jesus said to them, "Do not be afraid; go and tell my brethren to go to Galilee, and there they will see me." (Matthew 28:8-10)

To Two Disciples on the Road to Emmaus:

That same day two of Jesus' followers were walking to the village of Emmaus, seven miles from Jerusalem. As they walked along, they were talking about everything that had happened. As they talked and discussed these things, Jesus himself suddenly came and began walking with them. And he said unto them, These are the words which I spake unto you, while I was yet with you, that all things must be fulfilled, which were written in the law of Moses, and in the prophets, and in the psalms, concerning me. Then opened he their understanding, that they might understand the scriptures, And said unto them, Thus it is written, and thus it behooved Christ to suffer, and to rise from the dead the third day: And that repentance and remission of sins should be preached in his name among all nations, beginning at Jerusalem. And ye are witnesses of these things. And, behold, I send the promise of my Father upon you: but tarry ye in the city of Jerusalem, until ye be endued with power from on high. And he led them out as far as to Bethany, and he lifted up his hands, and blessed them, and he said unto them, These are the words which I spake unto you, while I was yet with you, that all things must be" *(Luke 24:13-50).*

To Peter (The First Time):

"The Lord has risen indeed, and has appeared to Simon!" (Luke 24:34)

To the Disciples (Without Thomas):

As they were saying this, Jesus himself stood among them, and said to them, "Peace to you. They were startled and frightened, thinking they saw a ghost. He said to them, "Why are you troubled, and why do doubts rise in your minds? Look at my hands and my feet. It is I myself! Touch me and see; a ghost does not have flesh and bones, as you see I have."

When he had said this, he showed them his hands and feet. And while they still did not believe it because of joy and amazement, he asked them, "Do you have anything here to eat?" They gave him a piece of broiled fish, [43] and he took it and ate it in their presence. He said to them, "This is what I told you while I was still with you: Everything must be fulfilled that is written about me in the Law of Moses, the Prophets and the Psalms."

Then he opened their minds so they could understand the Scriptures. He told them, "This is what is written: The Messiah will suffer and rise from the dead on the third day, and repentance for the forgiveness of sins will be preached in his name to all nations, beginning at Jerusalem. You are witnesses of these things. I am going to send you what my Father has promised; but stay in the city until you have been clothed with power from on high."

The Ascension of Jesus

When he had led them out to the vicinity of Bethany, he lifted up his hands and blessed them. While he was blessing them, he left them and was taken up into heaven. Then they worshiped him and returned to Jerusalem with great joy. And they stayed continually at the temple, praising God" (Luke 24:50-53).

To the Disciples (With Thomas):

The doors were shut, but Jesus came and stood among them, and said, "Peace be with you." Then he said to Thomas, "Put your finger here, and see my hands; and put out your hand, and place it in my side; do not be faithless, but believing." Thomas answered him, "My Lord and my God!" Jesus said to him, "Have you believed because you have seen me? Blessed are those who have not seen and yet believe." (John 20:26-29)

To the Seven Disciples:

After these things Jesus shewed himself again to the disciples at the sea of Tiberias; and on this wise shewed he himself. There were together Simon Peter, and Thomas called Didymus, and Nathanael of Cana in Galilee, and the sons of Zebedee, and two other of his disciples. Simon Peter saith unto them, I go a fishing. They say unto him, we also go with thee. They went forth, and entered into a ship immediately; and that night they caught nothing. But when the morning was now come, Jesus stood on the shore: but the disciples knew not that it was Jesus. Then Jesus saith unto them, Children, have ye any meat? They answered him, No. And he said unto them, Cast the net on the right side of the ship, and ye shall find. They cast therefore, and now they were not able to draw it for the multitude of fishes.

Therefore, that disciple whom Jesus loved saith unto Peter, It is the Lord. Now when Simon Peter heard that it was the Lord, he girt his fisher's coat unto him, (for he was naked,) and did cast himself into the sea. And the other disciples came in a little ship; (for they were not far from land, but as it were two hundred cubits,) dragging the net with fishes. As soon then as they were come to land, they saw a fire of coals there, and fish laid thereon, and bread. Jesus saith unto them, Bring of the fish which ye have now caught. Simon Peter went up, and drew the net to land full of great fishes, an hundred and fifty and three: and for all there were so many, yet was not the net broken. Jesus saith unto them, Come and dine. And none of the disciples durst ask him, **who art thou?** knowing that it was the Lord. Jesus then cometh, and taketh bread, and giveth them, and fish likewise. So, when they had dined, Jesus saith to Simon Peter, Simon, son of Jonas, lovest thou me more than these? He saith unto him, **Yea, Lord; thou knowest that I love thee**. He saith unto him, Feed my lambs. He saith to him again the second time, Simon, son of Jonas, lovest thou me? He saith unto him, **Yea, Lord; thou knowest that I**

love thee. He saith unto him, Feed my sheep. He saith unto him the third time, Simon, son of Jonas, lovest thou me? Peter was grieved because he said unto him the third time, Lovest thou me? And he said unto him, **Lord, thou knowest all things; thou knowest that I love thee.** Jesus saith unto him, Feed my sheep. Verily, verily, I say unto thee, when thou was young, thou girdest thyself, and walkedst whither thou wouldest: but when thou shalt be old, thou shalt stretch forth thy hands, and another shall gird thee, and carry thee whither thou wouldest not. This spake he, signifying by what death he should glorify God. And when he had spoken this, he saith unto him, Follow me. Then Peter, turning about, seeth the disciple whom Jesus loved following; which also leaned on his breast at supper, and said, Lord, which is he that betrayeth thee? Peter seeing him saith to Jesus, **Lord, and what shall this man do?** Jesus saith unto him, If I will that he tarry till I come, what is that to thee? follow thou me. Then went this saying abroad among the brethren, that that disciple should not die: yet Jesus said not unto him, He shall not die; but, If I will that he tarry till I come, what is that to thee? This is the disciple which testifieth of these things, and wrote these things: and we know that his testimony is true. And there are also many other things which Jesus did, the which, if they should be written every one, I suppose that even the world itself could not contain the books that should be written. Amen" *(John 21:1-25).*

To Five Hundred:

Then he appeared to more than five hundred brethren at one time, most of whom are still alive, though some have fallen asleep. (1 Corinthians 15:6)

To James and the Apostles:

Then he appeared to James, then to all the apostles. (1 Corinthians 15:7)

Before His Ascension:

Then he led them out as far as Bethany, and lifting up his hands he blessed them. While he blessed them, he parted from them and was carried up into heaven. And they worshiped him, and returned to Jerusalem with great joy, and were continually in the temple blessing God. (Luke 24:50-53).

To Stephen the First Martyr

But he, being full of the Holy Ghost, looked up stedfastly into heaven, and saw the glory of God, and Jesus standing on the right hand of God, and said, **Behold, I see the heavens opened, and the Son of man standing on the right hand of God**. Then they cried out with a loud voice, and stopped their ears, and ran upon him with one accord, And cast him out of the city, and stoned him: and the witnesses laid down their clothes at a young man's feet, whose name was Saul. And they stoned Stephen, calling upon God, and saying, **Lord Jesus, receive my spirit**. And he kneeled down, and cried with a loud voice, **Lord, lay not this sin to their charge. And when he had said this, he fell asleep**" (Acts 7: 54-60).

To Saul on the Road to Damascus

And Saul, yet breathing out threatenings and slaughter against the disciples of the Lord, went unto the high priest, and desired of him letters to Damascus to the synagogues, that if he found any of this way, whether they were men or women, he might bring them bound unto Jerusalem. And as he journeyed, he came near Damascus: and suddenly there shined round about him a light from heaven: And he fell to the earth, and heard a voice saying unto him, Saul, Saul, why persecutest thou me?

And he said, **Who art thou, Lord?** And the Lord said, I am Jesus whom thou persecutest: it is hard for thee to kick against the pricks. And he trembling and astonished said, **Lord, what wilt thou have me to do?** And the Lord said unto him, Arise, and go into the city, and it shall be told thee what thou must do. And the men which journeyed with him stood speechless, hearing a voice, but seeing no man. And Saul arose from the earth; and when his eyes were opened, he saw no man: but they led him by the hand, and brought him into Damascus. And he was three days without sight, and neither did eat nor drink" (Acts 9: 1-9)

To Ananias regarding Saul

"And there was a certain disciple at Damascus, named Ananias; and to him said the Lord in a vision, Ananias. And he said, Behold, I am here, Lord. And the Lord said unto him, Arise, and go into the street which is called Straight, and enquire in the house of Judas for one called Saul, of Tarsus: for, behold, he prayeth, And hath seen in a vision a man named Ananias coming in, and putting his hand on him, that he might receive his sight" (Acts 9: 10-16)

Historical Evidences of Belief in Resurrection

In the Book of Daniel in the Old Testament Daniel was given a vision and was then assured that he himself would be resurrected.

"And I Daniel alone saw the vision: for the men that were with me saw not the vision; but a great quaking fell upon them, so that they fled to hide themselves.

Therefore, I was left alone, and saw this great vision, and there remained no strength in me: for my comeliness was turned in me into corruption, and I retained no strength.

Yet heard I the voice of his words: and when I heard the voice of his words, then was I in a deep sleep on my face, and my face toward the ground.

And, behold, an hand touched me, which set me upon my knees and upon the palms of my hands.

And he said unto me, O Daniel, a man greatly beloved, understand the words that I speak unto thee, and stand upright: for unto thee am I now sent. And when he had spoken this word unto me, I stood trembling.

Then said he unto me, Fear not, Daniel: for from the first day that thou didst set thine heart to understand, and to chasten thyself before thy God, thy words were heard, and I am come for thy words.

But the prince of the kingdom of Persia withstood me one and twenty days: but, lo, Michael, one of the chief princes, came to help me; and I remained there with the kings of Persia.

Now I am come to make thee understand what shall befall thy people in the latter days: for yet the vision is for many days. (Daniel 10:7-14). And Daniel was given information on the future, some of which, he could not understand. Finally, the angel told Daniel, "But go thou thy way till the end be: for thou shalt rest, and stand in thy lot at the end of the days" (Daniel 12:2)

The Historical Record

The Jewish historian Josephus, (writing roughly in the same period as Paul and other authors of the gospels, Matthew, Mark, Luke, and John) wrote that the Essenes believed the soul to be immortal, so that while the body would return to dust the soul would go to a place fitting its moral character, righteous or wicked.

Jesus, defended the resurrection in His exchange with the Sadducees: "Those who are accounted worthy ... to the resurrection from the dead neither marry nor are given in marriage, for they ... are equal to the angels and are children of God" (Mark 12:24–25, Luke 20:34–36).

The **post-resurrection appearances of Jesus** provide eye witness evidence of his resurrection and His identity is confirmed through His being seated in Heaven on the right hand of God.

These appearances are confirmed by Luke in the book of Acts. "To whom also he shewed himself alive after his passion by many infallible proofs, being seen of them forty days, and speaking of the things pertaining to the kingdom of God" (Acts 1:3).

Faith

Will we be like the thief on the right of the cross? He certainly did not understand why suffering was allowed to occur on earth. Yet he acted in faith Will we, like this thief, also have faith for eternal salvation?

The Thief's account: "And he said unto Jesus, Lord, remember me when thou comest into thy kingdom. And Jesus said unto him, Verily I say unto thee, Today shalt thou be with me in paradise" (Luke 23: 42-43).

Jesus, as he suffered, with His statement, confirmed that eternal life exists. This account also confirms that eternal life is available to absolutely anyone who comes by faith regardless of the past. The thief did not have time to go to church, be baptisted, confirmed, or make attrition for his actions. He simply placed his trust in the redemptive work being done by Jesus Himself who cried out from that cross, "Father, forgive them; for they know not what they do" (Luke 23-34). Faith does not go by 'sight'. "Faith is the substance of things hoped for, the evidence of things not seen" (Hebrews 11:1)

Finally, before 500 people, the last time Jesus appeared on earth physically, "While they beheld, he was taken up; and a cloud received him out of their sight" (Acts 1:9).

Misunderstandings

Many people take offence to Jesus Christ's statement, "I am the way, the truth and the life, no man cometh to the Father but by me" (John 14:6).

They argue that there are many ways to God, and that there CANNOT be just one way to God! They exclaim that there are too many religions and beliefs and these all have value; therefore, it is wrong to say that there is only one 'way' that is the right way. They maintain ALL people can come to God any way that they choose, and that God is a God of Love and accepts all different religions and all people who come to Him. My response is, you are correct: "God is Love" (1 John 4:8). And it is certainly correct that 'whosoever shall call upon the name of the Lord shall be saved' (Romans 10:13). You are also correct, that the denomination, religion, or belief system is not a barrier to the Lord. However, we only have one person that has been raised from the dead who has been seen by over 500 people when a cloud circled His feet and He was taken up into heaven (Acts 1:9). And this **same Jesus, which is taken up** from you **into heaven, shall so come in like manner as ye have seen him go into heaven**" (Acts 1:11).

Neither is **there** salvation **in** any other: for **there is none other name under** heaven **given** among men, whereby we must be saved" (Acts 4:12).

Some have told me that Christians are responsible for the murder of many people, that many people have been killed because of religion. But historical evidence documents that it is actually Jews and Christians who have been killed by the governments and by religious denominations made by man for declaring faith in God and in Jesus Christ. The message of the Bible is one of 'Relationship" with God out of love for Him for His mercy, grace and love. "We love him, because he first loved us" (1 John 4:19)

Not invited:

What would we think if you were having a birthday, and someone arranged a Birthday party for you, and everyone came to celebrate and have a good time, but agreed that when 'you' got to the party, you would not be allowed to enter! Their fear was that your very presence would mean that everyone present would not be able to 'have a good time"? This is, in effect, what happens when we post a 'no entrance' sign on anything that is related to the Bible. Decisions are made to not believe

that the Bible is relevant, or necessary, or worthy to read. Comments I receive include: "I have tried to read the Bible, but it makes no sense to me". "Reading the Bible is a waste of time, I cannot understand any of it." "The Bible is full of killing, and hatred and Judgment – I do not want to be judged, I have done nothing wrong, I am a child of God and am created by God who is loving and kind and would not make anyone suffer." "Who would ask that their Son 'die'? – that is not a God I want to serve." "I cannot believe because there is not enough evidence for me to have faith, or make any determination." "I do not have any faith, because I choose to not have faith. I want to live my life!" I get to do what I want to do – this is MY life!" "Things are going just fine for me I don't need to believe in God." "I don't want to be viewed as a Jesus nut!"
Indeed, God has granted us 'free will choice'. We are FREE to live and act as we please while we are on earth in physical bodies. My goal is not to remove anyone's 'free will choice'. My purpose is to simply inform those I love and care about what the Lord has done for me. I am truly grateful that the Lord made it possible for me to come as a child with 'childlike faith' in a God who created everything, who has prepared a heaven which is beyond human imagination and who has assured us His Word is true.
"These things have I written unto you that believe on the name of the Son of God**; that ye may know that ye have eternal life, and that ye may believe on the name of the Son of God"** (1 John 5:13)

Chapter 23

Vessels Only

If a man therefore purge himself from these, he shall be a vessel unto honor, sanctified, and meet for the master's use, prepared unto every good work.
2 Timothy 2:21

We were created to be united with the Lord and to be obedient to His leading. In effect, to be a 'vessel' available for His use. There is plenty of work to be done. The question is, "Are we consecrated and dedicated to live a life as an available vessel?" The Lord can use any 'thing' and any 'one' to help us to understand and move forward.

We are created to 'serve' the Lord, rather than to have the Lord 'serve' us. *"Do not store up for yourselves treasures on earth, where moth and rust destroy, and where thieves break in and steal. But store up for yourselves treasures in heaven, where neither moth nor rust destroys, and where thieves do not break in or steal; where moths and vermin do not destroy, and where thieves do not break in and steal"* for where your treasure is, there will your heart be also* (Matthew 6:19-21).

The desire of my heart for my fifth wedding anniversary was to find a documentary to watch that would be inspirational for my husband Fabien and myself. As I looked through what was 'free' and available, I spotted, "Harry and the Snowman". This true account would have an amazing impact upon myself, my family, my friends, and Fabien's family.

"Harry and the Snowman" features the true story of Harry deLeyer's family with historical film clips and pictures. Harry and his wife became

For Such a Time as This?

immigrant from Holland who were invited to come to America after WWII by an American family for whom Harry had taken the time to bury their son. When the family found out what had been done, they invited Harry and his wife to come to America to work on their cotton farm. Harry began to bring their horses to races. Harry was told he had potential as a racer and that he should be on a horse farm. He worked and saved, and was able to move his family to Rhode Island to work on a horse farm. Once there, he decided he would go to the auction to see if he could get a riding horse for a small amount of money. He was delayed, and arrived too late to bid at the auction, but was just in time to see them loading 'unwanted' horses onto trucks to go to become 'dog' food. Harry went to see those horses, and spotted a white work horse on a truck. He asked them to take that horse off the truck and then he asked if he could buy him. He purchased the horse for $80. Once back at the horse farm, Harry and his children cleaned him up. The children decided to call the horse 'Snowman"! Snowman was a family horse, and was used to pull sleds, as well as a diving board. Snowman liked to swim! Harry had promised to sell the first horse he got to his neighbor for their son. He had sold another horse before snowman but not to his neighbor. Now, Snowman was the first horse that he had after that that was good with kids, so he sold Snowman. But within 3 days, Snowman travelled 6 miles to get back to Harry. The neighbor added a wire on top of the fence, but Snowman jumped the fence to return again to Harry. They put a tire on his leg to keep him from getting out. But Snowman returned again, this time with the tire on his hoof along with part of the fence. So, the neighbor sold Snowman back to Harry. Harry then promised Snowman that he would never sell him again.

Harry now knew that Snowman could jump fences. Harry decided to ride him to see if he could be taught to jump professionally. Snowman was a workhorse with big feet, but he could jump! In the end, Snowman won three Triple Crowns of Jumping, and then won every race he was entered in for 10 years. Harry and Snowman traveled the world. Snowman set a new record for the high jump that lasted for 10 years. Snowman even learned to jump over another horse. Snowman was totally yielded and obedient. When Snowman got old, he started to miss jumps. Harry let him retire. Then there came the day that Harry had to put Snowman down. Harry and Snowman had bonded, so this was sad. Harry buried Snowman on his property. Then, Harry continued to train horses. Ten years later, Harry, now older, trained a different horse, and won another Triple Crown of Jumping!

The account of Snowman made me remember my own dedication of my life to the Lord when I was 23 years old. After the film, I made another declaration to the Lord. "Lord, I am rededicating myself to you! I want to be like Snowman – help me to learn to become obedient to your every desire." The very next day, Fabien and I were asked to dinner by one of his sons, Chris. When we entered the home, the table was set. When I put my purse down, I noticed there was a hippopotamus sitting on a placemat on the table. I asked, "What is a hippo doing on your table?" Bobbie replied, "That is for you! We found the hippo at a flea market and when we saw it, we just had to get it for you." As I looked at the hippopotamus, I immediately saw that this hippo's head was down and turned to the right, and I thought immediately of Snowman. I replied, "We just watched the movie "Harry and the Snowman" and the hippo's head is exactly the same as Snowman's head was when he was taken off the truck. Bobbie trains horses, and replied, "When a horse puts their head down and turns it like that, it is a position of submission." As I listened, I knew this was confirmation from the Lord that He had heard my re-consecration prayer. I asked, "What exactly, did you go to the flea market to get?" Bobbie replied, "We went to find 4 stools for our new island that Chris made." I was stunned, and replied, "You don't need to continue to look for stools, I have them and will bring them to you. My sister's son, offered me 4 stools a few weeks ago, and I am sure he must still have them." When we got home, I contacted my sister. She was able to get the stools out of her son's storage and bring them to us, and we delivered them to Bobbie and Chris that very week.

This was a complete synergy of answered prayers. We all had been "vessels' that the Lord used: Bobbie with her purchase of the 'hippo' that provided me with confirmation of my prayer; my family gifting the stools to me, and me in turn gifting the stools to meet Bobbie and Chris's family's need for them!

Jesus Christ, as our Master, is able to help us to jump over the obstacles put in front of us, when we are yielded and obedient –even as Snowman was able to jump each hurdle that was placed in front of him!

(The picture on the back of this book is of that Hippo with a Snowman.)

Channels Only – Mary E. Maxwell, published 1900's

How I praise Thee, precious Savior,
That Thy love laid hold of me;
Thou hast saved and cleansed and filled me
That I might Thy channel be.

Channels only, blessed Master,
But with all Thy wondrous power
Flowing through us, Thou canst use us
Every day and every hour.

Just a channel full of blessing,
To the thirsty hearts around,
To tell out Thy full salvation,
All Thy loving message sound.

Emptied that Thou shouldest fill me,
A clean vessel in Thy hand;
With no power but as Thou givest
Graciously with each command.

Witnessing Thy power to save me,
Setting free from self and sin;
Thou who bought me to possess me,
In Thy fullness, Lord, come in.

Jesus, fill now with Thy Spirit
Hearts that full surrender know,
That the streams of living water
From our inner man may flow.

PRAYER: Lord, thank you that **YOU** *are* **GOD**, and that **YOU ARE able** to do abundantly, above and beyond all that we can ask or think!

Help us to come to you with open hearts and hands, that we may live in harmony with one another, and with your precious Holy Spirit.

Chapter 24

The Key

"Trust in the LORD with all thine heart; and lean not unto thine own understanding. In all thy ways acknowledge him, and he shall direct thy paths. (Proverbs 3: 5-6)

The Key:

It is quite ironic that a simple 'key' can start a vehicle that can transport us where we desire to go, even if we understand very little of how the engine works, or how the drive shaft connects to transport us forward or reverse with just the move of a lever. We do not demand to have to understand pistons, radiators, to drive a car! Yet when it comes to having Faith in the Lord, such childlike 'faith' is totally unacceptable. We object! We demand to understand the 'how' and 'why', and willingly walk away without further consideration because 'faith' does not agree with how we think or with what our minds believe to be true.

In truth, the reason most of us object has nothing to do with Jesus or having faith. The main reason is because the message of Jesus is one of 'not my will, but Thine be done."

The immediate response has been, "No one can tell me how to live my life!" Or, "I want to just enjoy life!" Contained within the statements is a 'belief' that whatever Jesus is offering is something 'horrible' and not to be desired because it may require some 'sacrifice' that we are NOT willing to make.

The truth is that Jesus is our Heavenly Friend. He is "a **friend that sticketh closer than a brother**" (Proverbs 18:24). Even when we are pushing Him and His Holy Spirit away.

Who, in their right mind, does not recognize the benefit of having a good friend?! And how many times do we need to talk to someone: to tell them about something bothering us, or share a joy with them?

If earthly friends can offer such comfort, what makes us believe that The Lord Himself who created us, is NOT GREATER than any earthly friend?! And who in their right mind would not want to be friends with the God who made the universe, who dispatches angels to help and aid us?!

Relationships take time. Being a friend to someone takes energy and love for them.

The truth is:

The truth is that in our innermost heart, we 'miss' our fellowship with God, and that is what makes us want to do all those crazy things, that 'spend us' and leave us feeling just empty, and wanting more. **The ways of this world CANNOT satisfy our 'eternal soul'. We were created for higher things. The truth is, it is only when we 'give' that we truly 'receive'.**

"Give, and it shall be given unto you; good measure, pressed down, and shaken together, and running over, shall men give into your bosom. For with the same measure that ye mete withal it shall be measured to you again" (Luke 6:38).

The truth is, it is when we are willing to 'go that extra mile' and 'stretch ourselves' that we really connect with each other and with God. That is what we were created for. The idea that living a life of simple pleasures and consumption of material wealth will satisfy us is actually the very first lie told to us by a fallen Angel Lucifer who left his first estate with that very same expectation of fulfillment:

"Ye shall not surely die: For God doth know that in the day ye eat thereof, then your eyes shall be opened, and ye shall be as gods, knowing good and evil" (Genesis 1:3 & 5).

The same fallen Angel offered Jesus the world without having to suffer at all! "Again, the devil taketh him up into an exceeding high mountain, and sheweth him all the kingdoms of the world, and the glory of them; And saith unto him, All these things will I give thee, if thou wilt fall down and worship me" (Matthew 4:8-9).

Heaven is to Come:

Should we have even just one 'glimpse' of heaven, there would be no one who would proclaim themselves an atheist, or agnostic, or an agnostic atheist, or that "I'm all set". But the reality is, if we **did** have that one glimpse of Heaven right NOW our God given 'free will' would be compromised. Then, we would run to God, because that vision would create within us a desire to **not miss out** on being able to be a part of the amazing reality of a perfect place that goes on forever world without end.

"O Labor not for the meat which perisheth, but for that meat which endureth until everlasting life, which the son of man shall give unto you: for him hath God the Father SEALED" (John 6:27).

"Precious in the sight of the Lord is the death of His saints" (Psalm 116:15).

"And I give them eternal life, and they shall never perish, neither shall any man pluck them out of my hand. My Father, which gave them to me, is greater than all, and no man is able to pluck them out of my Father's hand" (John 10:28).

When we 'ask' Jesus to remember us, He will!

Once we have trusted Him for our salvation, His Holy Spirit that created and gave us life empowers us to become His witnesses on this earth to proclaim the good news. "And he said unto them, Go ye into all the world, and preach the gospel to every creature" (Matthew 16:15).

Teaching them to observe all things whatsoever I have commanded **you**: and, lo, **I am with you** alway, even unto the end of the world" (Matthew 28:20).

For Such a Time as This?

The saying, "For Such a Time as This?" comes from the book of Esther in the Bible. Esther is the only book of the 66 books in the Bible that does not contain the word "God". The book of Esther contains an historical account of what occurred during the reign of Xerxes who banished his wife Vashti from his presence during the seventh year of his reign (Esther 2:16).

During this time, the Israelites were in captivity in Babylon, their temple closed, and their prophets silent. Mordecai who was a Jew, took responsibility for raising Esther, a Jewish orphan who became the Persian queen to King Ahasuerus (Xerxes). [Their marriage would enable God to use Esther's step son Artaxerxes to provide Nehemiah with all the resources required to rebuilt the walls of Jerusalem (Nehemiah 2:1-8).]

For Such a Time as This?

Archeology confirms the Biblical account. In 1930, the palace of Xerxes was excavated and restored by the Oriental Institute of Chicago (pictures of the discovery are available on the internet).

Mordecai served the King and one of his actions saved the King's life. That act was recorded and read to the King, which made the King want to recognize him for his bravery" (Esther 2:21-23). Haman ascended to a position of power with the King. When Haman ended up being required to give honor to Mordecai for that act, Haman was enraged. "Haman the son of Hammedatha, the Agagite, the enemy of all the Jews, had devised against the Jews to destroy them, and had cast Pur, that *is*, the lot, to consume them, and to destroy them" (Esther 9:24). Then Haman convinced the King to sign an edict that required the extermination of all Jews as rebels to the King.

"Then were the king's scribes called on the thirteenth day of the first month, and there was written according to all that Haman had commanded unto the king's lieutenants, and to the governors that were over every province, and to the rulers of every people of every province according to the writing thereof, and to every people after their language; in the name of king Ahasuerus was it written, and sealed with the king's ring" (Esther 3:12).

When Mordecai who was a Jew, as was Esther, learned of the signing of the degree (Esther 3:6), he sent notification to Esther with a message, "And who knoweth whether thou art come to the kingdom **for such a time as this?**" (Esther 4:1-3).

Queen Esther responded, "Go, gather together all the Jews that are present in Shushan, and fast ye for me, and neither eat nor drink three days, night or day, I also and my maidens will fast likewise, and so will I go into unto the king, which is not according to the law: and if I perish, I perish" (Esther 4:16).

Esther's brave act of faith in seeking God through fasting and prayer was recognized by God. The evil plot of Haman was worked for 'good'. The day of the planned execution of the Jews, is now celebrated as the Feast of Purim". By FAITH, we too can move those 'mountains' of 'sight'.

"There is always one thing to do – do what is right and leave the rest with God. Prayer moves the hand that moves the world. God's pioneers leave all - to gain all." Henrietta Mears "What the Bible is All About"

The world is rapidly approaching the days of fulfillment of Bible prophecy regarding the return of the Lord in the air for His own, known as the rapture.

"For the Lord himself shall descend from heaven with a shout, with the voice of the archangel, and with the trump of God: and the dead in Christ shall rise first: Then we which are alive and remain shall be caught up together with them in the clouds, to meet the Lord in the air: and so, shall we ever be with the Lord" (1 Thessalonians 4:16-17).

"And this **gospel** of the kingdom **shall be preached** in **all the world** for a witness unto **all** nations; and **then shall the end come**" (Mathew 24:14).

COMMIT TO GOD

If you cannot remember a time when you have verbally acknowledged to the Lord that you believe Jesus Christ came, that he died, and that He is risen, and have accepted His payment for your 'sins' – talk to Him and ask Him, just like the thief on the cross, **"Remember me when I come into your Kingdom!" – Please forgive me and write my name in Your book of life".** Stop and do that **right now**! You do not have to wonder, guess, or hope about whether you will be in heaven. Jesus came and bled and died to make payment for the sins of the entire world. God raised Jesus from the dead in order that ALL would choose and accept God's FREE GIFT of salvation. "These things have I written unto you that believer on the name of the Son of God; **that ye may KNOW that ye have eternal life**; and that ye may believer on the name of the Son of God: (1 John 3:13).

BECOME KNOWLEGEABLE

Find a Bible believing church in your area and visit a service, or a Bible Study. Make time to read the New Testament account of the life of Jesus Christ for yourself. Designate a time to read the Bible each day. The Bible is available via the computer, Tablet, and the 'old fashioned' way, from a Bible. My preference is to read a King James Version (KJV) Bible that is large print where I can make notes and underline passages that speak to my heart. I highly recommend marking a hard copy of the Bible with underlines, and highlights. The book of Luke is the easier to read. Stop and think about what you are reading and what it means to you right now. God's Words to us have 'power and 'life' from God's Holy Spirit. These words allow us to 'grow' in our knowledge of God, and of the true value of our life. God sent Jesus to us, to show us how to live our life with concern and care for one another. Jesus Christ lived a life of "LOVE" in action. He was not passive or silent. He lived what He taught. Jesus prayed to His Father every day. How can we not do the same? He taught us the "Our Father".

BE PRAYERFUL

Make time after reading the Bible, to pray about things happening in your day. Talk to the Lord like you would talk to a friend. Ask Him not only to protect and keep you and your family and ask Him to allow you the privilege of being useful to Him, to see and recognize opportunities to share His love with others. This can be as simple as picking up the phone and calling or texting someone who is on your mind, or to write a note to encourage someone you love. It always makes my day to receive a 'card' or 'note' in the mail unexpectedly.

BE READY

After I committed my life to the Lord, my gratitude for my salvation and awareness of the brevity of life, caused me to desire to encourage others. I purchased poems and mini Bibles and mini-animals and created small bags that I now carry with me and offer to those who help me or that I see doing their job well – to thank them for their service. We live in challenging times, but **GOD IS IN CONTROL** – He has promised to work it all things for our good! (Romans 8:28). Those who refuse to have FAITH, walk by SIGHT, and can be discouraged by the evil in our world. We are told that human hearts will grow 'cold' due to the evil in our world as we approach the time of the return of the Lord in the air. "And because iniquity shall abound, the love of many shall wax cold" (Mathew 24:12). Therefore, let us heed these powerful words:

"May the objects of my life's pursuits be worthy of an immortal Spirit worthy of an heir of Heaven. Deliver me from whims and hobbies and nerve me for the infinite possibilities which are opening up before me." Charles H. Spurgeon – "Flowers"

"He Is no fool who gives up what he cannot keep to gain what he cannot lose." Jim Elliot 1949 Martyred Christian Missionary to Ecuador

PRAYER:

Lord, empower us with Your divine energy for each moment of our day. Help us to obey your leading. Help us to pray. Help us to seek your will for our lives. Help us to be like Esther!

Help us to walk in faith, to fast, to pray, to thank you and to Praise You! Help us Lord, for your name's sake, to be believers who choose to work and to wait and to listen and to follow the leading of your precious Holy Spirit, just as Esther did, ***'for such a time as this?"***

Collectively we as believers must turn back to the Lord in FAITH, because that is what he is going to be looking for when He returns: FAITH in practice, daily, hourly, often in the common place moments of our life.

When we think of someone, stop and say a prayer for them. The moments when we are 'interrupted' we need to stop what we are doing, and see, and then do what needs to be done.

This is our moment, **"For such a time as this!"**

Old Testament Prophecies of Jesus Christ Foretold:

Genesis 3:15	First promise 4000 BC
Genesis 49:10	Time of His first coming
Isaiah 7:14	How are we to know Him
Genesis 21:12	He must be of Abraham's seed
Micah 5:2	Where he will be born – 710BC
Isaiah 9:6	He will be God – the everlasting father 742 BC
Daniel 7:13	He will be the Son of man
Malachi 3:1	John the Baptist will prepare His way
Isaiah 49:6	He will be a savior to the Gentiles as well Jews
Isaiah 35:4-6	he will heal the sick and broken hearted
Isaiah 61:1-3	He will set the people free
Psalm 78:1-3	How He will preach
Zechariah 9:9	He will ride into Jerusalem on a donkey 487 BC
Isaiah 53	Suffer untold agonies
Psalm 22:16	They will pierce His hands and feet
Psalm 22:17	They will cast lots for His garments
Zechariah 12:10	He will be crucified and pierced
Psalm 22:1	He will appear to be forsaken by God
Psalm 34:20	Contrary to custom none of His bones will be broken 1000 BC
Daniel 9:26	His death will be for others
Psalm 16:10	After resurrection He will ascend on High
Psalm 110:1	To sit at the right hand of God

You may go to Heaven:

Without **health**,

Without **wealth;**

Without **fame**,

Without a **great name**;

Without **learning**,

Without **earnings;**

Without **culture**,

Without **beauty;**

Without **friends**,

Without ten thousand other things . . .

BUT you can't go to Heaven WITHOUT CHRIST.

"Neither is there salvation in any other: for there is none other name under heaven given among men, WHEREBY WE MUST BE SAVED" (Acts 4:12) (Read: John 3, Romans 3, Ephesians 2)

FROM: SOWERS OF SEED, INC, P.O. Box 6217, Ft. Worth, TX 76115

Bible Promises of the Return of Jesus Christ to Earth:

This same Jesus, which is taken up from you into heaven, shall so come in like manner as ye have seen him go into heaven. Acts 1:11

For the Lord himself shall descend from heaven with a shout, with the voice of the archangel, and with the trump of God: and the dead in Christ shall rise first: Then we which are alive and remain shall be caught up together with them in the clouds, to meet the Lord in the air: and so shall we ever be with the lord. 1 Thessalonians 4:16-17

The Disciples ask: Tell us, when shall these things be? And what shall be the sign of thy coming, and of the end of the world?

And Jesus answered and said unto them, Take heed that no man deceive you. For many shall come in my name, saying, I am Christ; and shall deceive many. And ye shall hear of wars and rumors of wars: see that ye be not troubled: for all these things must come to pass, but the end is not yet.

For nation shall rise against nation, and kingdom against kingdom, and there shall be famines, and pestilences, and earthquakes, in divers' places. All these are the beginning of sorrows. Then shall they deliver you up to be afflicted, and shall kill you: and ye shall be hated of all nations for my name's sake.

And then shall many be offended, and shall betray one another, and shall hate one another. And many false prophets shall rise, and shall deceive many. And because iniquity shall abound, the love of many shall wax cold. Matthew 24: 3-12

And this gospel of the kingdom shall be preached in all the world for a witness unto all nations; and then shall the end come. Matthew 24:14

For then shall be great tribulation, such as was not since the beginning of the world to this time, no, nor ever shall be. And <u>except those days should be shortened</u>, there should no flesh be saved; but for the elect's sake <u>those days shall be shortened</u>. Then if any man shall say unto you. Lo, here is Christ, or there; believe it not. For there shall arise false Christs, and false prophets, and shall shew great signs and wonders; insomuch that, if it were possible, they shall deceive the very elect. Behold, I have told you before. Wherefore if they shall say unto you, Behold, he is in the desert; go not forth: behold he is in the secret chambers; believe it not.

For as the lightning cometh out of the east, and shineth even unto the west; so, shall also the coming of the Son of man be. Matthew 24:21-27

But of that day and hour knoweth no man, no, not the angels of heaven, but my Father only.

But as the days of Noah were, so shall also the coming of the Son of man be. For as in the days that were before the flood they were eating and drinking, marrying and giving in marriage, until the day that Noe entered into the ark, and knew not until the flood came, and took them all away; so, shall also the coming of the son of man be. Matthew 24: 36-39

Watch therefore: for ye know not what hour your Lord doth come. Therefore, be ye also ready; for in such an hour as ye think not the son of man cometh. Matthew 24:42, 44

Denying ungodliness and worldly lusts, we should live soberly, righteously, and godly, in this present world; Looking for the blessed hope, and the glorious appearing of the great God and our Savior Jesus Christ. Timothy 2:12-13

Are you ready to meet Christ should He come today? You can be, if you are willing to accept Jesus Christ as your personal Savior.

The Provision of God: Salvation in Christ

But God commendeth his love toward us, in that, while we were yet sinners, Christ died for us. Romans 5:8

Who his own self bare our sins in his own body on the tree, that we, being dead to sins, should live unto righteousness: by whose stripes ye were healed. 1 Peter 2:24

He that believeth on the Son hath everlasting life; and he that believeth not the Son shall not see life; but the wrath of God abideth on him. John 3:36

Jesus saith unto him, I am the Way, the Truth, and the Life: no man cometh unto the Father, but by Me. John 14:6

Nether is there salvation in any other, for there is no other name unto heaven given among men, whereby we must be saved. Acts 4:12 - And the blood of Jesus Christ His Son cleanseth us from all sin. 1 John 1:7

The Prayer of Confession: That if thou shalt confess with thy mouth to the Lord Jesus, and shalt believe in thine heart that God hath raised Him from the dead, thou shalt be saved. For with the heart man believeth unto righteousness, and with the mouth confession is made unto salvation. (Romans 10:9-10) Whosoever therefore shall confess me before men, him will I confess also before my Father which is in heaven. (Matthew 10:32)

The Power Available for the Christian Life

This I say then, walk in the Spirit, and ye shall not fulfil the lust of the flesh. Galatians 5:16 For God hath not given us the spirit of fear, but of power, and of love, and of a sound mind. 2 Timothy 1:7

But as it is written, eye hath not seen, nor ear heard, neither have entered into the heart of man, the things which God hath prepared for them that love Him. But God hath revealed them unto us by his Spirit; for the Spirit searcheth all things, yea, the deep things of God. 1 Corinthians 2:9-10

These things I have spoken unto you, that in Me ye might have peace. In the world ye shall have tribulation; but be of good cheer; I have overcome the world. John 16:33

RESOURCE: Radio Bible Class (RBC) Ministries is a great resource for understandable and accessible information about Jesus Christ and His Holy Bible. To learn more on how to be ready for His return, visit: http://rbc.org/

If you enjoyed, "For Such a Time as This? I would love to hear from you: Dawndensmore@gmail.com **For more inspiring information visit:**www.GodsAmazingWays.com

Other books written by Dawn Densmore-Parent
DIVINE ENCOUNTERS: The Reality of God, Angels and Demons
Experiencing God's Amazing Ways
Experiencing God's Precious, Priceless Promises
To order this book visit: Amazon.com or visit Kindle eBook's

www.ingramcontent.com/pod-product-compliance
Lightning Source LLC
Chambersburg PA
CBHW060157050426
42446CB00013B/2865